OSPREY AIRCRAFT OF THE ACES® • 52

Sopwith Camel Aces of World War 1

SERIES EDITOR: TONY HOLMES

OSPREY AIRCRAFT OF THE ACES® • 52

Sopwith Camel Aces of World War 1

Norman Franks

OSPREY
PUBLISHING

Front cover
Few Sopwith Camels carried more than the basic national insignia and perhaps a very limited personal marking to add to squadron identification markings. The exceptions were the Camels flown by the Royal Naval Air Service (RNAS), which used colours and patterns to identify its pilots in the air. This particular aircraft, Camel B6358, was used by 10 Naval Squadron after having first served with the Seaplane Defence Squadron at Dunkirk in 1917. Passed on to 9 Naval Squadron following its service on the French coast, B6358 was transferred to 10 Naval Squadron in February 1918. It was regularly flown by Flt Sub-Lt Lawrence P Coombes whilst with the latter unit, the future 15-victory ace claiming his first two kills with B6358. The veteran fighter was eventually sent to the RAF's No 213 Sqn in June, and was shot down on 25 August by German Marine ace Oberflugmaat Christian Kairies, this being his fifth kill.

This specially commissioned cover artwork by Iain Wyllie depicts the aircraft during its service with 10 Naval Squadron in early 1918, its blue and white horizontal stripes and wheel covers, as well as the letter 'C', revealing its assignment to the unit's 'C Flight'. 'A Flight' used black and white stripes on its Camels and 'B Flight' red and white. The white vertical stripes on the aircraft's fuselage were exclusively used by 10 Naval Squadron after August 1917. Finally, the wheel cover designs varied from fighter to fighter, but they were always in flight colours. The RNAS reverted back to Royal Flying Corps control in February 1918, and following the formation of the RAF on 1 April that same year, this Camel would have lost its nose colours. Indeed, with 10 Naval Squadron being redesignated No 210 Sqn, the unit's identification marking became a far more subdued white disc behind the fuselage cockade

First published in Great Britain in 2003 by Osprey Publishing
Elms Court, Chapel Way, Botley, Oxford, OX2 9LP

ISBN 1 84176 534 1

Edited by Tony Holmes
Page design by Tony Truscott
Cover Artwork by Iain Wyllie
Aircraft Profiles by Harry Dempsey
Scale Drawings by Mark Styling
Index by Alan Thatcher
Origination by Grasmere Digital Imaging, Leeds, UK
Printed in China through Bookbuilders

03 04 05 06 07   10 9 8 7 6 5 4 3 2 1

EDITOR'S NOTE
To make this best-selling series as authoritative as possible, the Editor would be interested in hearing from any individual who may have relevant photographs, documentation or first-hand experiences relating to the world's elite pilots, and their aircraft, of the various theatres of war. Any material used will be credited to its original source. Please write to Tony Holmes at 10 Prospect Road, Sevenoaks, Kent, TN13 3UA, Great Britain, or by e-mail at; tony.holmes@osprey-jets.freeserve.co.uk

ACKNOWLEDGEMENTS
The author wishes to thank Mike O'Connor, Greg VanWyngarden, Stuart Leslie, Phil Jarrett, C G Jefford MBE and Andrew Kelly for their help in ensuring the completion of this title. The work of Ray Sturtivant and Gordon Page in their book *The Camel File* (Air Britain) is also acknowledged, as well as Chaz Bowyer's *Sopwith Camel - King of Combat* (Aston).

For a catalogue of all Osprey Publishing titles please contact us at:

Osprey Direct UK, PO Box 140, Wellingborough, Northants NN8 2FA, UK
E-mail: **info@ospreydirect.co.uk**

Osprey Direct USA, c/o MBI Publishing, 729 Prospect Ave, PO Box 1, Osceola, WI 54020, USA
E-mail: **info@ospreydirectusa.com**

CONTENTS

A PUGNACIOUS FIGHTER

While it is well known that the Sopwith F 1 Camel fighter appeared in operational squadrons after the Pup and Triplane in sequence, and before the Snipe, it is not so well known that the F 1 prototype had in fact arrived on the scene as early as December 1916. This was only a short while after the Pup had become operational with the Royal Naval Air Service (RNAS), and before it had started service with the Royal Flying Corps (RFC).

In late 1916, with the introduction of the German *Jagdstaffeln*, or *Jastas*, the German fighter pilots began to receive machines which carried twin synchronised machine guns. This meant that the Pups that began arriving on the Western Front in late 1916, and the Triplanes which followed, were already out-gunned as each type only carried one synchronised Vickers 0.303-in machine gun. Therefore, Sopwith's new F 1 design at least matched the German Albatros and Halberstadt fighters that were now in France opposing, with deadly effect, the airmen and aircraft of the RFC and RNAS.

The first Pups were sent to 8 Naval Squadron in October 1916, a unit with a mixed complement of aircraft (Pups, Nieuports and Sopwith 1¹/₂ Strutters), and these aircraft were almost immediately asked to help out the hard-pressed RFC on the Somme front by providing fighter support. Pups later equipped 3 Naval Squadron in early 1917, while the RFC finally took Pups on operations with No 54 Sqn in late December 1916, followed by No 66 Sqn in March 1917.

The Sopwith Triplane had also begun to arrive in France in late 1916, following trials with 1 Naval Squadron, and this unit was also drafted in to help the RFC in February 1917. Soon afterwards 8 Naval Squadron began exchanging its remaining Pups for the new Triplane.

'Bloody April' 1917 saw the German *Jasta* pilots cut a massive swathe through both RFC and RNAS ranks, and it was obvious that better fighter types had to be produced to combat their runaway success. New fighters were being promised, among them the Bristol F 2b Fighter, the SE 5 and the Sopwith F 1, now named the Camel because of its distinctive 'hump' over its two Vickers 0.303-in machine guns.

All three new types, in time, were to give the Allied airmen in France the superiority they required to support the land battles of late 1917 and 1918, although this took time, energy and combat experience. Indeed, the latter point was certainly a factor in the successful employment of the Bristol Fighter, for No 48 Sqn initially used it defensively and suffered terrible losses. It was only when its crews flew the F 2b offensively that it became the deadly opponent which many German pilots tried to avoid. The SE 5 too wrote its own history in the air war, but it was perhaps the Camel which became the most well-known of all the British fighters of World War 1, just as the Fokker Dr I triplane became the best known of the German fighters.

———— THE CAMEL ENTERS SERVICE ————

It is a fact that although the RNAS was created to support the Royal Navy and help defend British shores with floatplanes and seaplanes, the Admiralty, encouraged by its fighting airmen, were not slow in equipping units with fast, modern fighters. Thus, as the RFC in France became hard pressed once the land war became bogged down, the RNAS fighter units were available to support it. The Sopwith Company was a main supplier of aircraft to the RNAS, which is why the Pups, Triplanes and, initially, the Camel were built for them, and although the RFC used the Pup, it did not use the Triplane. The 'Corps had been interested in the type – it could use any modern fighter it could get its hands on – but in the end it was agreed that it was more expedient to transfer a naval order of French SPAD VIIs to the RFC and leave all the Triplanes to the RNAS.

The Camel, a design by Herbert Smith of Sopwiths, came together through the efforts of a team of Sopwith men. Designed specifically to house two guns up-front, firing through the propeller, the scout bore some resemblance to the Pup, although the design team decided to have the main mass weight positioned right up front, with the engine, guns/ammunition, pilot, fuel and oil tanks all housed within the first third of the fuselage. This gave it a rather squat, bullish appearance.

Another identifying feature was the wings. The upper-wing, to assist production, was made in one piece, perfectly straight with no dihedral, while the lower wings had increased dihedral. Ailerons were fitted to upper and lower wings, making the whole structure very manoeuvrable, especially with a 130-hp Clerget engine as its powerplant. This large rotary engine (that is to say the whole engine went round with the propeller), which rotated clockwise when viewed from the cockpit, together with the mass frontal weight gave the Camel a massive right-hand turn capability.

This in itself was fine for pilots once they had gained experience on the type, but in the beginning it came as a shock, especially to pilots coming off docile training types, or service machines like the Pup. The Camel's nose tended to drop during a steep turn to starboard (with the rotating engine), and for it to rise with a port climbing turn (against the rotating engine). In both cases the pilot had to put on left rudder.

Sir Leslie Hollinghurst (later an Air Chief Marshal) was awarded a DFC in 1918 whilst flying Sopwith Dolphins in France (a rare Sopwith in-line engine design), but flying initially with the Aircraft Acceptance Park at Kenley, he had gained a good deal of experience on Camels. He once told me that he had to go to a training station in the Midlands as pilots on Camels were writing themselves off at an alarming rate. Once there he quickly saw the problem, as the embryo pilots, when trying a loop, simply pulled back on the stick and waited, as they had done with more submissive types, for the machine to complete the up-and-down circle. The Camel did not let the pilot do this, and he explained to the trainees that one had to keep the engine running at full power and 'fly' it through the loop using full rudder.

Lt Alexander MacD Shook of 4 Naval Squadron claimed the first Camel victories on 5 June 1917, flying N6347. He survived the war with 12 victories to his name, as well as the DSO, DSC and CdG

Capt Noel Webb MC and Bar of No 70 Sqn made the first RFC Camel claims on 17 July 1917. A further eight kills would come his way in the next few weeks, boosting Webb's tally to 14 victories, prior to him being killed by Werner Voss on 16 August 1917 (*E F Cheesman*)

By May 1917 the first Camels were ready for France, and a batch went to equip 4 Naval Squadron, operating from Bray Dunes, north of Dunkirk, gradually replacing its Pups. The first recorded encounter with the enemy came on the evening of 5 June, when Flt Cdr A MacD Shook attacked and claimed an Albatros D III destroyed and a two-seater shot down 'out of control' over Ostend, both in Camel N6347. There was, apparently, a fight the previous afternoon in which Shook is also thought to have engaged a two-seater which he forced down off Nieuport – no official record exists of this engagement, however.

Alexander MacDonald Shook was a Canadian from Ontario, born on 2 December 1888. Aged 28, he was older than most of his contemporaries. Shook flew Sopwith two-seater Strutters during 1916 with 5 Wing, before going to 4 Naval Squadron when it formed in April 1917 as a flight commander. His victories on 5 June 1917 made him an ace, for he had previously scored three victories with the Sopwith Pup during April and May. Shook would continue to fly with 4 Naval Squadron until the spring of 1918, although he was wounded on 21 October. By mid-March 1918 he had scored 12 victories altogether, which brought him the Distinguished Service Cross (DSC), then the Distinguished Service Order (DSO) and the *Croix de Guerre* (CdG). As a major in the new RAF, created on 1 April 1918 with the amalgamation of the RFC and RNAS, Shook added an Air Force Cross to his awards. He died in Bala, Ontario, on 30 May 1966.

One of Shook's more unusual victories was a Gotha bomber destroyed on 4 July 1917. With 4 Naval Squadron based on the North Sea coast, the unit was strategically placed to intercept raiders heading for England, and on this day he and another pilot engaged several Gotha bombers at 0830 hrs north-west of Ostend. Shook reported that the aircraft he had fired at had gone down smoking and with one engine stopped. However, the Germans did not admit any losses, and there is a question as to whether his claim was fully acknowledged.

The second RNAS squadron to equip with Camels was No 6 Naval Squadron at Flez, which then moved to Bray Dunes having given up its Nieuport Scouts for Camels in late June. As the year progressed, Camels went to 3, 8 and then 9 Naval Squadrons. 10 Naval Squadron also became a Camel outfit by replacing its Triplanes and 12 Naval Squadron received Camels as well. This latter unit was in fact something of an 'operational training unit/pilot pool', pilots being posted here from England for a final 'polish' before going to a frontline squadron as vacancies occurred. Another unit on the French coast was the Seaplane Defence Squadron (formerly the St Pol Defence Flight), which flew Pups. Its previous aircraft had been Sopwith Baby, Sopwith Schneider and Short 184s, hence the 'Seaplane' element of its name. It became 13 Naval Squadron in January 1918 and received Camels.

By then, the first RFC squadron designated to receive Camels had been operating the type for almost six months. No 70 Sqn, at Boisdinghem, near St Omer, had until mid 1917 been operating two-seat 1½ Strutters. The first Camel arrived on 13 June, and it was fully equipped by July. Capt C F Collett scored the unit's premier victory with the F 1 when he downed an Albatros D V Scout on 27 June flying B3756. The next claim was made 15 days later when N W W

Webb brought down an Albatros C X of *Flieger Abteilung* 18 over British lines at Bellevue while he was performing an air test. The C X was captured intact and given the British serial G.51. By coincidence Webb was flying B3756 on 12 July, this aircraft having been used by Collett to score the first RFC Camel kill.

Then, in a scrap to the south of Gheluvelt on the evening of the 17th, a patrol led by Capt Webb encountered Albatros Scouts. Webb sent down two 'out of control', Lt E Gribben another, Lt J C Smith a fourth and Capt F H Laurence a fifth. This fight was against Manfred von Richthofen's *Jasta* 11, and one German pilot was wounded.

The first RFC pilot to claim a victory with the Camel, Clive Franklyn Collett was born on 28 August 1886 in Blenheim, New Zealand. He joined the RFC in 1914, but a crash halted his operational progress. Collett flew as a test pilot instead, with one of his tasks being to experiment with a parachute, jumping from a BE 2c two-seater! Once with No 70 Sqn in France he became a flight commander, and his first Camel victory was also his first claim. By early September Collett had 11 victories and the Military Cross (MC) and Bar, but on the 9th he was wounded in the hand during a fight with *Jasta* 35b. Returning to test piloting in England, he was at the controls of a captured Albatros Scout when the machine broke up in flight over the Firth of Forth on 23 December 1917 and he was killed.

Another early Camel ace with No 70 Sqn was Noel William Ward Webb from Kensington, London, although he was born in Margate on 12 December 1896. He joined the RFC in March 1916, and by July he was flying FE 2b 'pushers' with No 25 Sqn, gaining five victories with his observers. Webb soon received the MC, and after a period at home, became a flight commander with No 70 Sqn in June 1917. He continued in action throughout the summer of 1917, gaining a Bar to his MC, but on 16 August, with his score at 14, he was shot down and killed by the German ace Werner Voss – his 37th victory.

Two further Sopwith Strutter squadrons exchanged their two-seaters for Camels in July (No 45 Sqn) and September (No 43 Sqn). The Strutters had given good service but their time was now up in France.

THE NEW FIGHTER

Lt L H 'Titch' Rochford had flown Pups with 3 Naval Squadron, and gained three kills. I had the pleasure of meeting 'Titch' in the 1970s – a great little man. As his unit equipped with Camels in July 1917, he wrote of the engine problems with its Bentley 150 hp BR 1 motor;

'By the middle of July, the Camel had completely replaced our Pups. Although the Pup was a delightful little aeroplane to fly, the Camel was undoubtedly a much superior fighting machine. At first we had a considerable amount of trouble with engine seizures, or partial seizures, due to the breaking of a coil spring in the oil pump of the Bentley engine. Our CO happened to meet W O Bentley at Dunkirk and told him of our troubles, and later he brought him out to Furnes to show him the broken springs. Bentley took them back to England and soon returned with a supply of springs made from a different material. Every engine in the squadron had its oil pump taken apart and the new spring fitted to it, after which there was no more trouble.'

New Zealander Capt Clive Collett MC and Bar claimed 11 victories flying Camels with No 70 Sqn in the summer of 1917. Wounded in combat and sent back to the UK, he was eventually killed when the captured Albatros Scout that he was testing over the Firth of Forth broke up in flight on 23 December 1917

Top-scoring RNAS pilot in World War 1, Canadian Ray Collishaw claimed 60 victories. A third of these he downed whilst flying Camels with No 203 Sqn RAF

Collishaw used Camel D3417 to claim no fewer than 19 victories whilst with No 203 Sqn. Capt L H Rochford also claimed two victories with this machine as well

Leonard Henry Rochford came from Enfield, North London, born on 10 November 1896. He tried to join the RNAS when war began but was too young to be accepted, so instead he learnt to fly at Hendon in 1915 and was finally allowed into the service in May 1916. His first unit in France was 3 Naval Squadron. By the time Rochford started flying Camels he was an experienced fighter pilot, and by 1918 a flight commander in the unit, which had now become No 203 Sqn RAF. By the end of the war he had achieved 29 victories and won for himself the DSC and Bar and the Distinguished Flying Cross (DFC). He became an engineer and a farmer after the war, and in World War 2 again served in the RAF. He died on 17 December 1986, aged 90.

Ray Collishaw, one of the most successful naval pilots of the war, had already achieved 38 victories on Strutters, Pups and Triplanes by the time he moved on to the Camel when he took command of the Seaplane Defence unit, soon to become 13 Naval Squadron, in late 1917. He would command No 203 Sqn in 1918, also on Camels. I was fortunate enough to correspond with him in the late 1960s, for he was an ardent aviation historian. Of the Camel he wrote;

'The Camel was far heavier and more powerful than the Pup, and faster. It had none of the Pup's docile and forgiving manners, and with the Camel things could happen very quickly. The torque effect of the rotary engine caused the nose to drop on right-hand turns while it tended to rise on left-hand turns. Therefore, a spin could easily develop if a pilot made a tight, uncorrected turn.

'My first flight in a Camel came two days after joining the Seaplane Defence Squadron, and I found it to be a delightful aircraft. It was as much fun to fly as the Pup, but its overall performance and its armament gave you a feeling of confidence. I had my first taste of action with it on 30 November – a high offensive patrol (OP) over Bruges. We had two combats but neither resulted in anything decisive. The next day while on an OP over Zeebrugge, we attacked three German seaplanes and chased them down to 4000 ft. I got on the tail of one and sent it down, but I could not be sure whether it crashed into the sea or merely made a hard landing.

'On 19 December three of us were escorting DH 4s, spotting for our naval fire on shore targets, when we ran into a pair of Albatros two-seaters. One of my pilots, George Mackay, from Sunderland, Ontario (18 victories), followed one of them down as it dived towards Zeebrugge and fired two bursts at it. The observer stood up in his cockpit holding up both arms, and then fell right out of the machine which went down out of control. The other two-seater got away, but then met up with a formation of four Albatros fighters and I was able to take one of them by surprise, sending it down out of control.'

Raymond Collishaw was born on 22 November 1893 in British Columbia, Canada, and upon leaving school he became a seaman with the Royal Canadian Navy's Fishery Protection Service. In January 1916 he joined the RNAS and his first posting was to 3 Naval Wing on Strutters, gaining two victories during a bomb raid. Going onto Pups with 3 Naval Squadron, Collishaw downed two more German machines in early 1917, and then moved to Triplane-equipped 10 Naval Squadron. He commanded a flight with the latter unit, and by late July had a total of 38 kills and the DSC, followed by the DSO.

After leaving 13 Naval Squadron, Collishaw took command of No 203 Sqn RAF, and by the end of the war had been credited with 60 victories, He had also added a DFC and CdG to his medal total, as well as a Bar to his DSO. After the war he led the Camel Flight of No 47 Sqn in South Russia, adding one further victory to his tally and assisting in another, but mostly he was engaged on command duties as a lieutenant-colonel. Between the wars Collishaw saw service in Iraq and in the Sudan, also attending the RAF Staff College. During World War 2 he commanded the Desert Air Force's 201 Group and then 12 Group within Fighter Command in England. Collishaw retired as an Air Vice-Marshal CB OBE in 1943, and lived in Vancouver until his death in 1975.

Collishaw's No 203 Sqn, with the ace seated prominently in the centre in his distinctive naval 'blues'. To his left is 'Titch' Rochford DSC DFC (29 victories, 26 on Camels). To Rochford's left is E T Hayne (15 victories). On Collishaw's right is H F Beamish (11 victories), then A T Whealy (27 victories). In the front row, the first three from the left are W Sidebottom (14 victories), W A W Carter (1 victory) and J E L Hunter of No 204 Sqn (12 victories). Finally, at the far right of the front row is F J S Britnell (9 victories)

THE NAVAL SQUADRONS

1 Naval Squadron/No 201 Sqn RAF

Formed at Furnes, Dunkirk, in December 1916 from 'A' Squadron, 1 Wing RNAS (early naval squadrons were identified by letters rather than numbers), this unit was initially equipped with Sopwith Pups and French Nieuport Scouts. By January 1917 1 Naval Squadron was flying Sopwith Triplanes, and had moved to support the RFC on the British front. Eventually returning to the North Sea coast, then Dover, it converted to Camels in December of that same year. In February 1918, the unit once again came under RFC control, and on 1 April it became No 201 Sqn RAF. By war's end it had scored over 250 victories, and produced 18 aces.

The squadron's top Camel ace was the remarkable Samuel Marcus Kinkead, who was born on 25 February 1897 in Johannesburg, South Africa. He came to England and joined the RNAS in September 1915, becoming known either as 'Kink' or 'Sammy'. Kinkead saw action with 3 Naval Wing in the Dardanelles, where he was credited with three victories flying Bristol Scouts and Nieuports. Posted to Dunkirk in 1917, he joined 1 Naval Squadron, flying Triplanes, and by 12 November had claimed a total of nine victories. Following the unit's re-equipment with Camels, Kinkead's score increased to 14 by year end, and he returned to England for a rest. Back with 1 Naval Squadron in

Lt Sammy Kinkead, formerly of 1 Naval Squadron/No 201 Sqn, is seen seated in his No 47 Sqn Camel whilst in South Russia, fighting the Bolsheviks, in 1919. He survived World War 1 with 35 victories to his name, 26 of which were scored in Camels

March 1918, he continued to score throughout the year, by which time his unit had become No 201 Sqn, and his final tally was 32. By November 1918 the RNAS had given him the DSC and Bar and the RAF the DFC and Bar. Accompanying Ray Collishaw to South Russia in 1919-20 to fly Camels with No 47 Sqn, Kinkead achieved further kills (possibly as many as ten) against the Bolsheviks and received the DSO. Remaining in the RAF, he was a flight commander with No 30 Sqn, and between the wars saw action in Mesopotamia and Kurdistan. A part of the Schneider Trophy Team, he was killed when his Supermarine S 5 crashed on 12 March 1928.

Ronald Sykes won a DFC with No 201 Sqn and became a minor ace in 1918. In correspondence with me in 1971, he recalled one patrol led by Kinkead, whom he thought one of the best flight leaders he had flown with. Kinkead had signalled to Sykes to attack a Fokker biplane but once engaged he could not get the Fokker in his sights;

'I pulled up in a steep climbing turn towards my flight above, but as I did so down came Capt Kinkead, and he flashed past me onto the tail of the German machine. I half-rolled over and went down to protect Kinkead's tail, and as I gave a quick glance astern I saw that the general dogfight was on, with three of our Camels who had stayed up involved in circling matches among a lot of Fokkers.

'Kinkead and his German, with me just above them, kept together, circling, half-rolling, diving. I had a real bird's eye view of the deadly aerial combat between two of the most skilful of pilots, beginning at about 11,000 ft and ending at ground level. I do not think either of them ever got their gunsights lined up on their adversary on their way down, owing to the extraordinarily clever flying. I know that the German easily evaded the few attacks I made, so I kept to my duty of protecting my leader's tail, for during rearward glances I could see at first many machines circling above us.

'Finally, however, there was only the German and Kinkead below and ahead of me, almost at ground level and in a vertical bank, with the Fokker in front. Kinkead pulled hard back on his stick, and for a second got his guns to bear on the Fokker's rudder, which was hit and put out of action. The German levelled up and crash-landed unhurt not far from Bayonvillers among Australian troops.'

Stanley Wallace Rosevear came from Walkerton, Ontario, born on 9 March 1896, and he then grew up in Port Arthur. He joined the RNAS from Toronto University in January 1917, and by the early summer was flying Triplanes with 1 Naval Squadron. He gained eight victories before the Camels arrived, and by late April 1918 his score had risen to 25, which won for him the DSC and Bar. However, on 25 April, during a test flight in B6231, Rosevear failed to pull out of a dive on a practice ground target and was badly injured in the resulting crash. He died at 1130 hrs at No 19 Casualty Clearing Station. Fourteen of his Camel victories had come in B6428, but this partnership was broken on 22 April when Capt G A Magor was shot down and killed in it by ace Hans Weiss of *Jasta* 11 near Hangard.

Born on 21 July 1899, George Brian Gates came from Hove, Sussex, and when he joined the RNAS in June 1917 he was nearing his 18th birthday. By March 1918 he was with 1 Naval Squadron, flying

No 201 Sqn ace Ronnie Sykes DFC was often led into combat by Sammy Kinkead in 1918. Note that his DFC ribbon has been sewn onto his tunic in reverse

Camels, and by late September he had achieved 16 kills, and received the DFC and Bar. A wound eventually took Gates out of the frontline, but he was still one of the youngest flight commanders in the RAF. Nine of his victories came in F5941 'E', and Capt Ronnie Sykes DFC also used this Camel to achieve his sixth victory on 9 November 1918.

Reginald Carey Brenton Brading came from Croydon in Surrey, having been born on 4 May 1899 in nearby Addlestone. Joining the RNAS in May 1917, he went to 12 Naval Squadron in late 1917 and then moved to 1 Naval Squadron/No 201 Sqn. Brading's first victory came on 2 May 1918, and after gaining five kills he was promoted to flight commander. He ended the war with a score of 13 victories, plus the DFC and Bar. Immediately post-war Brading served in the Baltic fighting the Bolsheviks and received a Mention in Despatches. During 1921 he flew a Sopwith Snipe in the RAF's aerobatics team.

Maxwell Hutcheon Findlay came from Aberdeen, where he was born on 17 February 1898, although he spent his early life in Canada. When war came he joined the Black Watch, and later transferred to the RNAS. By 1917 Findlay was serving with 6 Naval Squadron on Camels, where he gained two victories, before moving to 1 Naval Squadron in the autumn. He became an ace on 8 March 1918, and by 30 May had achieved 14 victories and been awarded both the DSC and DFC. Seven of Findlay's kills were scored in B6419, and he was himself shot down in this aircraft on 6 April 1918 by *Jasta* 34's August Delling, thus becoming the first of the German's five victories.

After the war Findlay remained in the RAF, serving in Afghanistan and Waziristan, before retiring in 1921 to become a farmer. However, he remained in touch with flying as an instructor and sales manager with the Brooklands School of Flying in the 1930s, and was killed in a flying accident during the Johannesburg Air Race in October 1936.

British-born (15 January 1895) Cyril Burfield Ridley lived in Toronto pre-war and had gained four victories on Triplanes with 1 Naval Squadron in 1917. Moving over to Camels, he gained his 11th kill on 11 July 1918, having become an ace with his first Camel victory – a balloon – on 12 March. He shared the latter kill with fellow

Camel B6420 of 1 Naval Squadron was used by aces C B Ridley and R P Minifie. After claiming four Camel victories (his previous 17 had all been on Triplanes) with it, Minifie was shot down whilst at the controls of this machine on 17 March 1918. He spent the rest of the war as a PoW (*Bruce/Leslie collection*)

Triplane ace Charles Booker DSC commanded No 201 Sqn from March through to August 1918, claiming six Camel victories during this time to raise his tally to 29. He was shot down and killed on 13 August by 30-kill ace Ulrich Nester of *Jasta* 19, having downed three Fokker D VIIs just minutes prior to his demise

ace Herbert Victor Rowley (his sixth victory). Ridley subsequently received the DSC and became a flight commander, but after the war he was killed in a flying accident near Cologne on 17 May 1920. Rowley survived the war with nine victories, his last coming on the day 1 Naval Squadron became No 201 Sqn (1 April 1918). Four of his kills came on Camels.

Two other 1 Naval Squadron/No 201 Sqn Camel aces were Canadian James Henry Forman and Robert McLaughlin from Belfast. The former scored six kills with the squadron, a seventh Camel claim with 6 Naval Squadron, a solitary Triplane victory and a final Camel kill over an LVG two-seater whilst serving as a flight commander with No 70 Sqn on 10 August 1918. McLaughlin's six victories were all scored with No 201 Sqn between 9 May and 16 September 1918, resulting in him receiving the DFC.

Canadian Hazel LeRoy Wallace (born on 13 November 1897) from Manitoba became a Camel ace with two squadrons, claiming six victories with 1 Naval Squadron/No 201 Sqn and six more with No 3 Sqn RAF. Having previously made two claims whilst flying Camels with 9 Naval Squadron in September 1917, the 14-victory ace also received the DFC. He died on 22 March 1976.

Finally, Charles Dawson Booker, one of the RNAS's leading Triplane aces, was given command of 1 Naval Squadron in March 1918, having already achieved solitary Pup and Camel victories and 21 Triplane kills with 8 Naval Squadron. Flying with No 201 Sqn, Booker had added six more victories with the Camel by the time he was shot down by German ace Ulrich Neckel of *Jasta* 19 (victory 22 of 30) on 13 August 1918. Booker's wingman recorded that the RNAS ace had shot down three Fokker D VIIs prior to being killed.

3 Naval Squadron/No 203 Sqn

3 Naval Squadron pilots were an experienced bunch by the time the Camel arrived in June 1917. Formed in late 1916 at Dunkirk from 'C' Squadron of 1 Wing, the unit was strengthened by an influx of pilots from 3 Wing. Its Sopwith Pups in turn came from 8 Naval Squadron, which was in the process of converting to Triplanes. Operating in support and under the control of the RFC from February to May 1917, 3 Naval Squadron was one of the most successful fighter units at the front. With the arrival of Camels in June, it spent several months in England, but returned to France in January 1918 and became No 203 Sqn in April under the command of Ray Collishaw. With almost 250 claimed victories, the unit produced no fewer than 23 aces.

The squadron's leading Camel ace was 'Titch' Rochford, who we met earlier. His total of 29, of which 26 were claimed whilst flying the Camel, were scored between 4 March 1917 and 29 October 1918. Ray Collishaw, who we have also talked about, scored 19 Camel victories, plus two more with the Seaplane Defence Squadron and a couple more in South Russia in 1919. All of his No 203 Sqn claims were made in Camel D3417, which had previously been used by Rochford, and in which 'Titch' claimed two of his victories.

Canadian Arthur Treloar Whealy (born on 2 November 1893) came from Toronto, and his total of 27 victories included five with the Pup and two with the Triplane, and the remaining 20 with the Camel. He had begun his fighting career with 3 Naval Squadron, but had then spent some time with 9 Naval Squadron in the summer of 1917. Whealy's reward for his success was the DSC and Bar and the DFC. He was rested on 24 September 1918 and did not return to combat.

Whilst with No 203 Sqn, his main Camel was B7220, which he used to claim 14 of his victories. F C Armstrong claimed another kill in this machine and Bob Little got one as well before another pilot was shot down in it on 5 June 1918 during an engagement with MFJ 2.

James Alpheus Glen, yet another Canadian from Ontario, was born in June 1890 and flew with 3 Naval Squadron's 'B Flight', gaining five Pup victories. His first Camel kill came on 27 July 1917, but he then spent time in hospital. Returning to France with the squadron in January 1918, Jimmy Glen had increased his overall score to 15 by 11 April, the last six of these being claimed in B7185 – F C Armstrong also claimed a kill in this machine, and in June it was in an action which resulted in another claim. Glen received the DSC and Bar and CdG, and was then rested from May 1918. Post-war, he served with the RCAF until 1928, when he rejoined the RAF. Retiring from the air force in 1938, Glen eventually died in England on 7 March 1962.

Edwin Tufnell 'Bollocky' Hayne was born in South Africa on 28 May 1895. He joined the RNAS in 1916 and arrived at 1 Naval Squadron the following year. Hayne achieved 15 victories, all whilst flying Camels, which brought him the DSC and DFC, prior to him being rested in July 1918. At least seven of Hayne's victories were claimed whilst flying D3376. Having survived the war, he was killed on 28 April 1919 in a flying accident at Castle Bromwich. Squadronmate Len Rochford recalls his demise;

'Hayne was in "A Flight", and he served with 3 Naval Squadron for about a year. After he left to return to Home Establishment, he was killed in an accident. He took off in a Bristol Fighter and the engine cut out. He tried to turn back to the aerodrome with the all too familiar result – a stall followed by a dive to earth.'

Born in Manchester on 11 October 1893, William Sidebottom was an RFC man who was posted to No 203 Sqn in the early summer of 1918. All 14 of his credited victories were claimed on the Camel, the last eight of them in C197. Sidebottom duly received the DFC, and post-war he served with the RAF in South Russia.

Canadian Frederick Carr 'Army' Armstrong from Toronto (born on 19 June 1895) had joined the RNAS in 1915. One of the 3 Wing transferees into 3 Naval Squadron, he scored his first of five Pup victories on 6 April 1917. In July Armstrong took command of 'C Flight', and between 16 September and 24 March 1918 accounted for eight German aircraft whilst flying Camels. His overall tally of 13 victories gained him the DSC and CdG, but on 25 March he was seen to go down in flames south of Ervillers in B7218 after trench strafing.

Ten Camel victories, plus one flying a Pup, was the record for New Zealander Harold Francis 'Kiwi' Beamish, who was born on 7 July 1896. He had joined the RNAS in June 1916, and was posted to

3 Naval Squadron in early 1917, where he gained his first victory on 23 April. Once flying the Camel, Beamish had increased his score to 11 by 18 May 1918, for which he received the DSC. He returned to New Zealand on rest, but the war ended before he could return, and post-war he became a sheep farmer. He died on 26 October 1986. Beamish's last six claims were all in B3855, and his kills were certainly diverse – three Albatros D Vs, one D III, two Fokker Triplanes, one Pfalz D III, one seaplane, a DFW, an LVG and Rumpler two-seaters. Beamish once told me about the following incident;

'On one occasion, our flight became split up after a dogfight above thick clouds. When the ground at last appeared I was completely lost, so I landed in a field to try and find our where I was. I felt certain I was on the right side of he line, but was horrified to see men in German uniforms running towards me. You can imagine my relief as I then saw British Tommies appear, and later discovered that these Germans were prisoners. I was quickly told where I was, and had soon took off to fly back to our aerodrome. Quite a relief!'

Leonard Rochford also told me another story about 'Kiwi' Beamish;

'"Kiwi" was leading a formation of five Camels, of which I happened to be in one. On take off one of his wheels fell off, unknown to him, just as he became airborne. During the patrol we all tried to attract his attention by pointing at his undercarriage but without success. When we arrived back at the aerodrome another pilot was up with a big notice "Wheel Off" on the side of his Camel, but "Kiwi" did not see him either and went in to land. He made a perfect tail down landing and the Camel went up on its nose with little damage. Very lucky.'

Born on 3 July 1897, Aubrey Beauclerk Ellwood was the son of a vicar in Rutland. Educated at Marlborough, he joined the RNAS in June 1916, and in April of the following year he went to 3 Naval Squadron. However, he did not open his account against the enemy until the Camels arrived, shooting down a seaplane on 27 July off Ostend. By 9 April 1918 he had brought his score to ten, and received the DSC. Instructing for the rest of the war Ellwood remained in the RAF and attained the rank of air marshal, having been AOC of Coastal Command's 18 Group in 1943-44. Post-war, he spent time as Director General of Personnel, and was then AOC-in-C of Bomber Command between 1947 and 1950. Ellwood then headed Transport Command until he retired in 1952. Made a KCB in 1949, he died on 20 December 1992 in Somerset.

Another Camel ace to serve with 3 Naval Squadron was John Denis Breakey from Sheffield, who made nine claims in 1918 for which he was given the DFC and Bar. He too rose in rank, to Air

William Chisam of 3 Naval Squadron was credited with seven victories. He is seen here posing with a Pup

17

Vice-Marshal CB CBE, before passing away in 1966. Frederick John Shaw 'Duke' Britnall from High Wycombe also achieved nine victories in 1918 with this unit, winning the DSC and DFC, and Robert Alexander Little scored his last nine with No 203 Sqn, taking his score to 47. Bob Little's career is detailed in the 8 Naval Squadron section.

William Hargrove Chisam, from Carlisle, scored seven victories with 3 Naval before being wounded in the hand on 26 March 1918, and Louis Drummond Bawlf from Winnipeg 'made ace' with five victories on 22 July 1918. However, his brother David, also in No 203 Sqn, was killed in a flying accident on 21 April. Louis was so affected by this tragedy that he was posted home. He died in Toronto in August 1966.

4 Naval Squadron/No 204 Sqn

The top ace of this, the first Camel-equipped squadron of the RNAS, was Charles Robert Reeves Hickey, a Canadian from British Columbia, born on 10 September 1897. After service with the Canadian Mounted Rifles, he joined the RNAS, and by August 1917 was with 4 Naval Squadron. By the end of the year Hickey had scored two victories, and throughout 1918 he claimed steadily to bring his tally to 21 by 1 October, for which he received the DFC and Bar – eight of his claims were made in Camel C74. On 21 April he and Capt Keirstead forced down a two-seater of FA(A) 266 behind Allied lines near Wulpen. The ace landed nearby in order to try and keep Belgian civilians away from the machine, but it suddenly exploded, killing several people and injuring Hickey. On 3 October he collided with another pilot and was killed in the subsequent crash. His awarding of the DSO was announced on 2 November.

Born on 20 June 1895, Ronald McNeill Keirstead was also a Canadian, from Nova Scotia. He joined 4 Naval Squadron in June 1917, having learnt to fly at the Curtiss School in Toronto the previous year. Remaining with the unit until July 1918, Keirstead claimed 13 Camel victories during the first half of the year, which earned him a DSC. Six of his early kills were claimed in N6370 (also used by A J Enstone and A J Chadwick to score two victories apiece) while his last five came in B6389 (lost whilst being flown by another pilot on 13 July). During World War 2 Keirstead was with the Ministry of Munitions in the Canadian government, and he had his sight damaged following an explosion during a demonstration. He died on 23 October 1970.

With 13 Camel victories and four with the Pup, Albert James Enstone was the second highest scorer of 4 Naval Squadron. Born on 29 August 1895 in Birmingham, he joined the RNAS in April 1916 and was one of 4 Naval Squadron's original pilots in April 1917. His first Camel success (in N6347), and his fifth victory overall, took the form of a two-seat seaplane off Ostend on 7 July. Enstone remained active with the unit for over a year, by which time he had become a flight commander, received the DSC and then the DFC and, in addition to his 13 claims, had driven down a further 11 enemy aircraft. He returned to England in August 1918.

Canadian Ronald Keirstead DSC was credited with 13 Camel victories whilst serving with 4 Naval Squadron/No 204 Sqn between June 1917 and July 1918

Also a Canadian, William Craig DFC rapidly claimed eight kills with No 204 Sqn in August and September 1918. His run of success came to an end on 26 September when he was shot down and killed by a Marine pilot from MFJ 5

Australian George Gossip of 4 Naval Squadron/No 204 Sqn was credited with six Camel kills between October 1917 and July 1918. He died in Istanbul in 1922 (*Bruce/Leslie collection*)

John Ellis Langford Hunter (born on 31 January 1897) came from Tynemouth, Northumberland. Joining the RNAS in October 1916, he was posted to 4 Naval Squadron to fly Camels, gaining his first victory on 3 September. Two seaplane kills on 22 September ended his scoring for the year, and after a break, Hunter was back with the unit by late January 1918. Between then and mid-August he increased his score to 13, seven of which had been claimed in B3879 and five in B3894. On 12 August, in a fight in which he claimed three kills, Hunter was wounded in the leg while serving as a flight commander. Sent home to recuperate, he duly received the DFC for his work.

Adrian James Boswell Tonks, from London, finished the war with an even dozen Camel kills. Born 10 May 1898 in Kensington, he joined 4 Naval Squadron in August 1917, and stayed with this unit until rested in October 1918. He claimed four kills in 1917, and all his 1918 victories were over Fokker D VIIs. Awarded the DFC, Tonks was killed in a crash on 14 July 1919. Five of his claims were scored in Camel C66, which had previously served with 13 Naval Squadron (where it had been used to score three victories). Another No 204 Sqn pilot claimed the machine's ninth victory in September, but was shot down later that same month and its pilot taken prisoner.

Other Camel aces to serve with 4 Naval Squadron/No 204 Sqn included Arnold Jacques Chadwick from Toronto, six of whose 11 victories were on Camels, for which he received the DFC, and fellow Canadian William Benson Craig from Smith's Falls, Ontario. He claimed eight victories during August and September 1918 and also won the DFC, but was killed in action on 26 September in D3374 – the machine in which he had claimed six of his victories. Craig's victor was a Marine pilot from MFJ 5.

Robert MacIntrye Gordon from Glasgow gained nine victories and a DFC with No 204 Sqn in 1918. After the war he became a doctor, and in World War 2 he received the George Medal (GM) and DSO during service with the 51st Highland Division (as a lieutenant-colonel) in North Africa, Sicily and Italy. He was awarded the GM for rescuing two men from a burning vehicle during the Tunisian campaign in 1943. Gordon subsequently ran a medical practice in Braintree, Essex, and died on 19 April 1990.

Other pilots of note were Capt Charles Philip Allen, who was credited with seven Fokker D VIIs shot down in 1918, Henry

Almost certainly the youngest British ace of World War 1, Risden Bennett had claimed five kills with No 204 Sqn when he was shot down and killed during a raid on Zeebrugge on 28 September 1918. He was just 18 years and seven months old

Gordon Clappison, who destroyed six Fokkers, and was later an air commodore in the RCAF, and Australian George H D Gossip, who also achieved six victories between October 1917 and July 1918. He died in Istanbul in 1922. Thomas W Nash from Littlehampton, Sussex, achieved eight victories in 1918, became a flight commander and won the DFC, but was killed in action on 23 October, along with four other pilots from his flight. They were bounced by fighters from MFJ 2, led by Gotthard Sachsenberg, who took his own score to 28 following the fight.

Risden Mackenzie Bennett, born on 12 February 1900, was probably the youngest British ace of World War 1. The son of a surgeon from Beckenham, Kent, he attended Dulwich College and then joined the RNAS in December 1917. Assigned to No 204 Sqn in the summer of 1918, he had claimed five victories by mid-September, but on the 28th was shot down and killed during a raid on Zeebrugge in D8187 while still only 18 years old.

John Douglas Lightbody, a Scot from Hamilton, gained all five of his victories in October 1918 (in F3109), but was killed in action on 4 November (in F6257) during a scrap with *Jasta* 29. Osborne John Orr also claimed five victories in the summer and autumn of 1918, the American from Cleveland, Ohio, being killed in action in the disastrous fight with MFJ 2 on 23 October.

No 204 Sqn's markings worn on its Camels post March 1918 consisted of two white sloping bars in front of the tailplane, but later this was changed to a white triangle aft of the roundel. Individual aircraft were identified by numbers just aft of the cockpit.

8 Naval Squadron/No 208 Sqn

This unit was formed at St Pol in October 1916 with Pups, Nieuports and Sopwith two-seaters, but it soon standardised on Pups. Supporting the RFC, it converted to Triplanes in April 1917 and then to Camels, in flight rotation, in July-August that same year. The unit enjoyed a rest in England in March 1918, before returning to duty later that month and becoming No 208 Sqn RAF. By the end of the war its pilots had claimed nearly 300 victories, and 26 men had become aces.

Foremost among them was William Lancelot Jordan, a Londoner, although born in South Africa on 3 December 1896. He joined the RNAS as a mechanic in September 1916, then volunteered to fly as an air gunner. Eventually becoming a pilot, Jordan was sent to 8 Naval Squadron while it still had Triplanes, but the unit had converted to Camels by the time he scored his first victory on 13 July 1917. By the end of the year his tally had risen to eight, many of them shared kills, and all of the 'out of control' variety. A leg wound slowed him down in September, but by January 1918 he had fully recovered, allowing him to boost his total to 17 by the 28th of that month. Jordan had only added one more victory in February by the time the unit had moved back to England, where he received the DSC.

Returning to action with the newly redesignated No 208 Sqn, Jordan's claims reached 39 by 12 August. By then he had been

8 Naval Squadron's R J O Compston DSC and two Bars DFC added 15 Camel victories to the ten he had previously claimed with the Pup and Triplane. He served with this unit from late 1916 until the spring of 1918

R J O Compston's Camel B6340 'P' is seen parked closest to the camera in this line up shot of 8 Naval Squadron machines, taken in late 1917. He scored 13 of his 15 Camel victories with this aircraft (*Bruce/Leslie collection*)

awarded a Bar to his DSC, as well as the DFC. Rested from operations, he did not see further combat, and although he survived the war, he was killed in a car accident in the 1930s. Jordan flew a variety of Camels, with D1844 enjoying a run of seven victories in July 1918 and B6369 two in December 1917 and five in January 1918.

Australian Bob Little was already a Triplane ace by the time he started flying Camels, having made 24 claims with the earlier Sopwith whilst flying with 8 Naval Squadron, as well as three victories in the Pup. He enjoyed great success with the Camel, claiming ten kills in July 1917 alone, before moving to No 203 Sqn the following April. Nine of his 8 Naval Squadron kills were achieved flying N6378. Little's achievements brought him the DSC and Bar, then the DSO and Bar. He had increased his total to 47 victories with No 203 Sqn by the time he was brought down during a night action against a Gotha on 27 May 1918. Crash-landing, he bled to death from a bullet wound to the groin before he was found. Born in Melbourne on 19 July 1895, his score made him the most successful Australian fighter pilot in history. Little was married and had a baby son.

Robert John Orton Compston, the son of a vicar, was born on 9 January 1898, and serving in the RNAS, he went to 8 Naval Squadron in late 1916. His first ten kills came on Pups and Triplanes, and flying the Camel, he had raised his tally to 25 by mid-February 1918. Most of these were scored in B6340 (13 in all), and Compston won the DSC and two Bars, plus a DFC. In the summer of 1918 he led No 40 Sqn, but saw no combat. He served again in World War 2, and died on 28 January 1962. Compston wrote of his friend Little;

'Once Little came within range of an enemy he did not give up until 1.) the enemy was shot down, 2.) his own engine failed or 3.) he ran out of ammunition. He had in human guise the fighting tendencies of a bulldog – he never let go. Small in stature, keen-eyed and with face set grimly, he seemed the epitome of deadliness. Sitting aloft with the eyes of a hawk, Little dealt with death with unfailing precision. Seldom did he return to the aerodrome to report an indecisive combat, for as long as petrol and ammunition held out, Little held on until the enemy's machine either broke up or burst into flames.'

Edward Grahame Johnstone was another ace from London, born on 6 May 1899. He arrived at 8 Naval Squadron via 12 Naval Squadron, and made his first combat claim on 6 December. By the time 8 Naval Squadron became No 208 Sqn, Johnstone's score had risen to ten. After a rest, he remained in action until August, by which time he had received the DSC and brought his score to 17.

Johnstone once wrote about how the Germans operated, to some advantage to the Navy pilot;

'Until early 1918 it was possible to indulge in a certain amount of private warfare. That is to say that when the day's patrols were completed, one or two of the more experienced pilots were allowed to go off on their own, either to attack some announced objective or, more often, to lay in wait for some particular enemy machine which it might have been noticed formed a habit of crossing our lines or working at the same hour every day. It was curious how persistent was the German trait of working to a timetable, and how we were consistently able to shoot down two-seaters which habitually did the same thing at the same time. One would have imagined that after a while they would have arranged escorts or even laid traps for us, but although naturally we occasionally got the worst of the bargain, generally speaking these individual efforts were extremely successful.'

William Edward George Mann, born on 20 April 1899, was another youngster with No 208 Sqn. Known as 'Pedro' due no doubt to his dark looks, his 13 victories won him the DFC, and after the war he remained in the RAF and was something of a display pilot at air pageants. Mann eventually became an Air Commodore CB CBE, retiring in 1945, and in 1961 he retired from Decca Navigation Company after working in Beirut. His last years were spent in Hampshire, where he died on 4 May 1966.

Guy William Price was another 8 Naval Squadron ace who scored his victories – 12 – between December 1917 and February 1918. An Irishman known as 'Captain Kettle' because of his naval beard, he was born on 6 July 1895. He received the DSC and Bar for his exploits, but his career was cut short on 18 February during a strafing mission. Price was surprised from above by Theodor Rumpel of *Jasta* 23 and shot down and killed, becoming the German's fifth and final victory.

Canadian James Butler White also claimed 12 victories, between January and October 1918. Born on 7 July 1893 in Ontario, he won the DFC and was one of the few pilots to both identify and claim a Pfalz D XII, which looked very similar to the more common Fokker

Camel B6311 has its propeller swung in the winter of 1917-18. The aircraft was used by 8 Naval Squadron ace Guy Price to claim five victories during December 1917 and January 1918. Later passed on to 9 Naval Squadron/No 209 Sqn, B6311 achieved a sixth victory before being lost in action on 24 April (*Phil Jarrett collection*)

D VII – his D XII went down in flames on 6 September. After the war White became a stockbroker, and he died on 2 January 1972.

Harold Day, from Abergavenny, Wales, was born on 17 April 1897. His first unit was 10 Naval Squadron, equipped with Triplanes, and he claimed one victory with the type prior to moving to 8 Naval Squadron and Camels. Over the winter of 1917-18 he added ten more victories to his score, and won the DSC, but Day's luck ran out on 5 February 1918. Seen diving on a German fighter, his Camel seemingly broke up for no apparent reason and he fell to his death. A German pilot from *Jasta* 29 was quick to put in a claim for his fall.

Another ace to serve with 8 Naval Squadron was Reginald Leach Johns with nine kills. From Kilburn, London, he scored his victories between January and June 1918, but was killed in a flying accident on 11 July. John Sutherland McDonald also got nine after being the first pilot to be posted into the unit after it had become No 208 Sqn. His victories were accumulated throughout the year, and he ended the war as a captain. Richard Burnard Munday was another nine-victory ace, who was born in Plymouth but is believed to have spent time in Australia. The son of a Navy surgeon, he won the DSC with 8 Naval Squadron, scoring his victories between August 1917 and February 1918. He ended the war as a major.

Ronald Roscoe Thornley had seen action at Gallipoli with the Royal Naval Armoured Car Squadron, before moving to the RNAS in May 1916. Sent to 8 Naval Squadron in 1917, his first two claims were made in the Triplane, and by the time he left the unit in September he had added seven more with the Camel. Thornley's first victory with the latter type was a two-seater, which he brought down in company with R J O Compston over Lens. It fell into Allied lines, with a dead pilot and a wounded observer.

Pruett Mullins Dennett, was a Hampshire lad, born on 21 January 1899, and he had scored seven victories prior to being shot down by Kurt Schönfelder of *Jasta* 7 on 2 June 1918. Flying near the channel or North Sea coasts, pilots often encountered the German Marine fighter pilots, although Schönfelder was unique in being a naval pilot flying with the Army! Dennett was his ninth victim out of a total of 13. A pilot from No 210 Sqn shot him down before the month was out.

Rupert C D'A Gifford claimed six victories in 1918, as did Gerald K Cooper and Herbert H W Fowler. Fowler, a Canadian, suffered from ear trouble to the point where he almost lost his hearing in mid 1918, and had to leave the service. Post-war some of his hearing returned, and he lived till 1962. Two pilots claimed five kills, American Malcolm C Howell from Boonton, New Jersey, and Wilfred H Sneath from Hendon, North London. The latter pilot had just shared in the destruction of a Dr I on 6 April 1918 for his fifth victory when he was killed by Ltn Karl Hertz of *Jasta* 59. Sneath was the second of three victories Hertz would score before he too fell in combat on 9 May.

The markings worn by 8 Naval Squadron's Camels were the same as had been applied to its Triplanes – a white disc aft of the fuselage roundels. Once the unit became No 208 Sqn, the markings were changed to two white bars sloping outwards behind the roundel. Individual aircraft carried letters forward of the fuselage roundels.

9 Naval Squadron/No 209 Sqn

Formed at St Pol in February 1917 with the usual mix of Pups, Nieuports and Triplanes, this unit had been fully equipped with Triplanes by June, and was attached to the RFC until September. During this period it began re-equipping with Camels, and after a short rest in England, 9 Naval Squadron returned to France in March 1918. It had claimed 168 victories by war's end, and 17 of its pilots had 'made ace'.

Foremost amongst these was Joseph Stewart Temple Fall from British Columbia, who was born on 17 November 1895. Joining the RNAS in 1915, Joe became a pilot and went to 3 Naval Squadron, flying Pups, and he accounted for eight German fighters in the spring of 1917, followed by five more on Camels (all in N6364). On 30 August he was made a flight commander with 9 Naval Squadron, and over the next few months he racked up a further 23 claims, which brought his overall score to 36, 28 of them with 9 Naval Squadron (11 claims were made flying B3898). For these accomplishments Fall was awarded the DSC and two Bars. He remained in the RAF post-war, and by World War 2 was a group captain – the rank he retired with in 1945. Returning to Canada, Fall died on 1 December 1988, aged 93.

Sterne Tighe Edwards (born on 13 February 1893) was yet another Canadian ace, brought up in Carleton Place, Ontario. Firm friends with future naval aces Roy Brown and Murray Galbraith, he learnt to fly before joining the RNAS and became an original member of 3 Naval Wing in 1916. Flying with 2 Naval Squadron in early 1917, he achieved his first victory on the Sopwith Strutter on 1 March, but was wounded in the shoulder and both feet in the process. Transferring to fighters, Edwards served with 11 and 6 Naval Squadrons and finally 9 Naval Squadron from July 1917. By year end he had scored seven kills in Camels and won the DSC. Following a rest, he returned to France in February 1918, and by mid May he had increased his tally to 17, resulting in him receiving a Bar to his DSC.

All this took a toll on his health and he suffered a nervous collapse on 23 May, but recovered to become a flying instructor. However, Edwards was badly injured in a crash on 12 November 1918 and died ten days later. Six of his claims were whilst flying B6217, and his last eight while in B7199. Edwards successfully forced down two German aircraft behind Allied lines – a Rumpler two-seater of FA 23 on 12 April 1918 and a Fokker Dr I from *Jasta* 4 on 16 May.

Another ace with 16 Camel kills was Oliver William Redgate (born 23 November 1894) from Nottingham. Joining the RNAS in February 1917, he was with 9 Naval Squadron by the summer. It took him less than a year to make his mark, and win the DFC, although a serious leg wound on 15 May 1918 ended his operational career. Redgate served as an instructor until the Armistice.

An RFC veteran rather than a naval aviator, Robert Mordaunt Foster was the son (born on 3 September 1898) of a British Army colonel, and he initially served in the Royal Fusiliers. Moving to the RFC in June 1916, he first flew Pups with No 54 Sqn, with whom he gained a single one victory. Following a spell on Home Defence, Foster was assigned to No 209 Sqn, and his first victory came on 21 April 1918 – the day the unit was involved in the death of Baron Manfred von Richthofen. Seeing continual action until war's end, Foster increased his score to 16, and was awarded the DFC. He also forced down three German aircraft behind Allied lines – two C-types and the Fokker Triplane that S T Edwards was involved with.

Foster served in India and Iraq post-war, and in the early years of World War 2 was with Bomber Command. He subsequently held other commands in the Middle East, becoming AOC Desert Air Force in 1944. Retiring in 1954 as an Air Chief Marshal KCB CBE, and a Commander of the US Legion of Merit, Foster died on 23 October 1973. Eight of his claims came in B3838 and seven in C61, the former having previously been with 3 Naval Squadron (two victories) and the latter with No 203 Sqn (two victories) prior to Foster flying it with No 209 Sqn.

Harold Francis Stackard scored victories on Pups and Triplanes with 9 Naval Squadron, although 12 of his 15 were claimed with the Camel. From Muswell Hill, London, he was born on 2 March 1895 and had been to Charterhouse School. When war came he spent five months aboard HMS *Oratara* (part of the 10th Cruiser Squadron) as a subaltern in the Royal Naval Division, seeing action in France and then Gallipoli, before transferring to the RNAS in October 1916. Stackard eventually returned to France and spent eight months in the frontline with 9 Naval Squadron. Despite claiming two victories on Pups, one with a Triplane and the rest with Camels (most had been shared claims), he nevertheless appears not to have been decorated. By 1918 Stackard was instructing at Cranwell, and just prior to leaving the service he joined No 157 Sqn and flew the new Sopwith Salamander fighter. He had certainly had a long war.

Arthur Roy Brown, of course, will be ever famous for his service with 9 Naval Squadron, the Canadian being involved in the death of Baron

Fifteen-victory ace Harold Stackard claimed two kills on Pups, one with the Triplane and 12 on Camels, during eight months in France with 9 Naval Squadron in 1917. He scored four kills (and possibly two more) with this particular aircraft – Camel B3883 – in September 1917, and it was later used by high-scoring ace J S T Fall to down his 30th, 31st and 32nd victories in November of that same year

Stackard's Camel (left) reveals its upper wing rings in this photograph. The aircraft appears to be Camel B6327, which he used to claim his 15th and final victory on 27 October 1917. The Camel on the right is A W Wood's B3884

Roy Brown DSC and Bar of 9 Naval Squadron/No 209 Sqn

Thirteen-victory ace 'Wop' May DFC of No 209 Sqn

Camel B6398 had a long and distinguished career. It initially served with 1 Naval Squadron, where S M Kinkead claimed six victories with it in the winter of 1917-18. Later going to No 209 Sqn in May 1918, W R May scored his first two victories with it. By September B6398 was with No 201 Sqn, whose R C B Brading claimed four more victories flying it. Returned to the UK, the Camel was repainted as shown here, with the name *Sylvestre* under the cockpit, and flown from Gosport by Maj E L Foot MC as his personal machine (*Bruce/Leslie collection*)

Manfred von Richthofen on 21 April 1918. Born on 23 December 1893 in Carleton Place, Ontario, he too flew Pups and Triplanes before the Camel arrived. Brown had become an experienced flight commander by the time his unit became No 209 Sqn, and he had won the DSC. On the fateful 21 April, he had chased the 'Red Baron's' triplane as it sat behind 'Wop' May's Camel, chasing him back across the lines. Brown went to May's aid and tried to put the 'Baron' off his attack. Shortly afterwards, as von Richthofen, realising he had strayed too far over the Allied line, turned for home he was fatally wounded by ground fire and crashed.

Despite the controversy over who had fired the fatal shot, Brown received a Bar to his DSC, but a few days later he was forced to leave the squadron due to shot nerves and influenza. Back in England, he fainted in the air while instructing and was badly injured in the subsequent crash. Post-war, Brown became an accountant in Canada and also ran a small airline for a while. He died on 9 March 1944. In all he had been credited with nine or ten victories.

The man he had been trying to protect on 21 April had been fellow Canadian Wilfred Reid May from Alberta, born on 20 March 1896. He had known Brown in Canada, so was pleased to be posted to No 209 Sqn on completion of his flight training. Surviving the attentions of the 'Baron', he went on to become an experienced fighter pilot and flight commander, with 13 victories winning him the DFC. After the war, 'Wop' May became a test pilot for Canadian Airways, and also served in the RCAF Reserve. He became an OBE in 1934 and died in Provo, Utah, on 21 June 1952 while out on a hike with his family.

Yet another Canadian, Fred Everett Banbury from Saskatchewan (born 27 October 1894) had been a law student pre-war, and learnt to fly prior to joining the RNAS. Posted to 9 Naval Squadron, his first two victories were on Pups in the early summer of 1917, to which he had added nine more on Camels by March 1918, and received the DSC. On the day the unit became No 209 Sqn (1 April 1918), Banbury fainted in the air and died in the resultant crash. It is thought that he had in fact had a heart attack.

Arthur William Wood scored all 11 of his victories between early September and mid-December 1917. Born in Bradford, West

Yorkshire, on 9 April 1898, he joined the RNAS in October 1916. Eight of Wood's claims were achieved in September 1917, and all his victories were shared with other pilots – a feature of 9 Naval Squadron/No 209 Sqn's scoring and air fighting methods.

Another pilot involved in the 21 April encounter with the 'Red Baron' was American Oliver Colin LeBoutillier, known as 'Boots'. Born on 24 May 1894 in New Jersey, he joined the RNAS in Canada in August 1916. LeBoutillier's first four victories were scored with the Triplane, and he had increased his tally to ten with the Camel by the end of May 1918. After the war he became a skywriter in the USA and then a stunt pilot in Hollywood, taking part in 18 films. He also flew in the National Air Races and even gave Amelia Earhart her first dual flying instruction on twin-engined machines. In 1937 LeBoutillier joined the Civil Aeronautics Administration (CAA), and in World War 2 he was Inspector in Charge of the CAA in Wyoming and Colorado. Retiring to Las Vegas, he died on 12 May 1983.

Other aces with the squadron included Joseph H Siddall with nine kills, John K Summers and M S Taylor with eight, Cedric G Edwards with seven and Keith Mack Walker with five.

Lancastrian Joe Siddall was killed in action by Karl Degelow of *Jasta* 40 on 25 July 1918, and C G Edwards DFC, born in St Albans on 5 June 1899, was also killed, on 27 August 1918, when his Camel

Fred Banbury DSC had claimed 11 victories with 9 Naval Squadron by the time he was killed in a crash on 1 April 1918 – the day the RAF was formed. It is thought that the Canadian may have suffered a heart attack whilst aloft (*Bruce/Leslie collection*)

Six of Banbury's 11 victories were scored in Camel B6230 (*Bruce/Leslie collection*)

West Yorkshireman Arthur W Wood claimed 11 Camel victories in the last four months of 1917 with 9 Naval Squadron (*Bruce/Leslie collection*)

Wood used B3884 to down at least seven of his victories. The blue and white (edged in red) diamond shape on the fuselage was repeated on either side of the top wing centre section. This Camel later served with No 201 Sqn, 14-kill ace Max Findlay scoring two victories with it in 1918 (*Bruce/Leslie collection*)

Seven-kill Camel ace C G Edwards DFC of No 209 Sqn was killed in action on 27 August 1918 when his aircraft suffered a direct hit from a flak shell

(B6371) received a direct hit from a shell fired from the ground. Capts Summers MC and Walker were both downed by Lothar von Richthofen on 12 August 1918, Summers becoming a prisoner and Walker losing his life.

I was in contact with John Summers in the late 1960s – he retired to Rhodesia – and he sent me the following story;

'On 1 July 1918 we had one mighty scrap. There were four layers of Huns – "Tripehounds" on top, Fokker D VIIs below, Albatros Scouts below them and Pfalz Scouts at the bottom. It developed into one hell of a dog-fight and I fired at all kinds except the "Tripes". Three of us each shot down a Hun – I got an Albatros for my second victory. "Wop" May got a triplane and W A Stead another scout. We had lost one of our pilots that same morning in flames, his aircraft being seen to break up in the air, but now, several hours later, we still headed down into this mass of German fighters without, apparently, a care in the world. Were we lucky to come out? Probably, but it seemed perfectly normal to take on these odds without worrying too much.'

The markings for the squadron comprised, from August 1917, a white crescent (like a smile) behind the fuselage roundels, but the following month the aircraft began to have various decorative schemes, all of which were highly colourful. In March 1918 things became more regulated, and its Camels were identified with three vertical white bars, one ahead and two aft of the roundels. Some No 209 Sqn aircraft also had red cowlings and wheel covers.

10 Naval Squadron/No 210 Sqn

'Naval Ten' became famous long before the arrival of the Sopwith Camel, its pilots having done

Capt J K Summers MC of No 209 Sqn had claimed eight victories by the time he was brought down on 12 August 1918 (along with fellow No 209 Sqn ace K M Walker) by Lothar von Richthofen. He spent the rest of the war as a PoW

Capt Edwin Swale DFC and Bar was No 210 Sqn's leading Camel ace with 17 victories

exceptionally well with their Triplanes. It had been formed at St Pol in February 1917 with Sopwith 1$^{1}/_{2}$ Strutters and pilots from 3 Wing, then moved to Furnes to equip with Triplanes, which they used while under RFC control 'down south'. By the time the Camels arrived the naval pilots had slashed their way through the German Air Service, and Ray Collishaw's famous 'Black Flight' was well known. The cowlings and forward area of the fuselages had been painted black, and the Triplanes all had names such as *Black Maria, Black Roger, Black Prince* and so on. 'Naval Ten' scored around 50 victories with the Triplane.

The first Camel kills came in September 1917, and by war's end victories on all types were nearing 350. Some 29 aces had also been created, but at a price – 100 pilots had been lost since its formation.

Although Ray Collishaw was the unit's top ace, all his victories with 10 Naval Squadrons had come on the Triplane, so it fell to Capt Edwin Swale to be the unit's leading Camel ace with 17 victory claims between May and October 1918. 'Eddie' Swale was another youngster, born on 28 June 1899 in Chesterfield. He joined the RNAS in August 1917 and reached 10 Naval Squadron on 21 March 1918, just as the German Offensive began. He later commanded 'A Flight' and won the DFC and Bar before being rested on 21 October.

Swale was much in evidence in his home town post-war, helping with the family business, local politics, the town council and becoming Mayor in 1953. He was also a glider pilot and instructor with the Derbyshire and Lancashire Gliding Club, and at one time held the record for height – 7000 ft. In World War 2 Swale served as a wing commander with the 'Ultra' code-breakers, and with the 2nd Tactical Air Force, and was Mentioned in Despatches three times. His son Duncan was a Mosquito pilot who won the DFC in 1944. Still gliding in the 1950s, Swale became an OBE in 1964 and died in August 1978.

Lawrence Percival Coombes was a close second to Swale in the scoring stakes. Born in India on 9 April 1899, he joined the RNAS in June 1917 and went to 10 Naval Squadron via 12 Naval Squadron in late January 1918. He made his first claim just before his outfit became No 210 Sqn RAF, and by the end of July he had scored 15 kills and won the DFC. In a big fight on 26 June, he, Ken Unger and Ivan Sanderson accounted for four enemy aircraft, one of which was flown by the ace Kurt Schönfelder of *Jasta* 7, who had shot down P M Dennett of No 208 Sqn on 2 June (the German's last victory on 21 June had also been over a pilot from No 210 Sqn).

After the war Coombes went into barnstorming, before completing an engineering degree and then working with the RAE at Farnborough, the Marine Aircraft Experimental Establishment at Felixstowe and, in 1927, with the Schneider Trophy team during the Venice races. In 1938 he went to Australia to work for the government in aeronautical research, and in 1960 was seconded to the UN, becoming chairman of the Commonwealth Advisory Aeronautical Research Council and chief supervisor at the Aero Research Labs. He died in Melbourne on 2 June 1988.

In correspondence with Lawrence Coombes in 1972, he told me;

'On 11 May 1918, a patrol of 24 British and Australian Camels did a high offensive patrol. We dropped 92 bombs on Armentières, and set

No 210 Sqn's second-ranking Camel ace with 15 kills was Lawrence Coombes DFC

fire to an ammunition dump. About eight enemy aircraft dived on us and about 20 more attacked at our level. There was a general dog-fight, one Australian Camel going down in flames while Alexander of '210 got an enemy aircraft also in flames. I shot down an Albatros out of control. Turning for home, we discovered that a ground mist had suddenly come up, covering a huge area of France. Nine of our Squadron crashed – including myself – trying to land in fields, one pilot being killed and another severely injured. Quite a number of Allied aircraft were taken by surprise and suffered similar fates.'

American ace Kenneth Russell Unger from Newark, New Jersey, was born on 19 April 1898. He joined the RFC because he had been turned down by his own US Air Service, despite having had flight instruction and holding a US Aero Club Certificate! He therefore travelled to Canada to join up in June 1917. By the time Unger reached France the RAF had been created, hence his joining No 210 Sqn. He claimed 14 kills – eight Fokker D VIIs, a Pfalz D XII, a Triplane, two Pfalz Scouts, a Halberstadt C-type and a balloon – which netted him the DFC. Unger's first claim, shared with Coombes and Sanderson, was against German ace Karl Schönfelder of *Jasta* 7 on 26 June 1918. In fact in that first successful combat, he was involved in the downing of four aircraft. Unger's first real combat had occurred three days earlier;

'Nine of us went over the lines last evening in three formations of three machines each. One Hun dove at us from above, so we turned and our leader (Coombes) shot him down in flames. When they turned I lost track of our formation and stayed up above, flying in big circles to see if I could find them again. I looked around and saw three Hun machines about 500 ft above me and about 300 yards behind me. I watched them, as I knew I was in for a hot time of it as one of the machines was a triplane, which is the Hun's best machine. They dove at me and I flew straight until I heard his gun open fire. I then did a sharp right-hand turn which brought our machines nose to nose. I opened fire with my guns and the triplane went down in a nosedive for about 500 ft, then climbed again. I turned and opened fire again but they beat it off as my two squadronmates came up with another three formations to help out.

'On our way back to our lines we spotted seven Huns after our third formation so we turned and attacked them. Two of us dived at one machine and fired about 50 rounds apiece into him and he went down and crashed. Our little formation had had three scraps in one hour and thirty minutes and had two machines to our credit. We had quite good fun and a lot of excitement while it lasted.'

If this was *Jasta* 7 they were up against then the triplane would no doubt have been flown by Josef Jacobs, its leader and star pilot, who much preferred flying the Dr I to the D VII, and did so for the rest of the war. Therefore, Unger was lucky to survive the encounter, Jacobs having claimed 21 of his eventual 48 victories by this stage of the war.

After the war Unger flew with the US Air Mail service, operating between Salt Lake City, Utah, and Oakland, California, before becoming a pilot with the Johnson & Johnson Company. In World War 2 he flew cargo aeroplanes with the US Navy, attaining the rank of lieutenant commander. Unger died in Florida on 6 January 1979. He had flown all his life, and survived a bale-out in 1932 due to his aeroplane breaking-up in the air during a display at Hadley airport, New Jersey, where he had started a flying school.

Canadian William Melville Alexander from Toronto (born on 8 November 1897) was already an eight-kill ace on Triplanes when he started flying the Camel. His ninth victory came on 16 August in one of the first Camels issued to 10 Naval Squadron, although he reverted to the Triplane for his next two kills. The unit had completed its re-equipment with the Camel by year end, and by May 1918 Alexander had boosted his tally to 23 victories (13 on Camels and ten on 'Tripes'), and he had also received the DSC. He returned to live in Toronto after the war, where he died on 4 October 1988. In an interview in 1970 he recorded;

'I learned to fly at the Stinson School in San Antonio, Texas, in November 1915. I was only 17, and deemed too young to go overseas. However, by November 1916 I was in France with 3 Wing.

'At the end of August 1917 I went home, leaving the Triplanes. When I got back we had Camels, and they had broken up 6 Naval Squadron. We had about six pilots and our casualties were so bad that they couldn't remake it with replacements. So they broke up 6 Naval Squadron, gave us their Camels and sent our "Tripes" to No 1 Sqn.

'The Camel was one of the finest machines I ever flew, but when a young pilot initially went up in one he had to be awfully careful for the first 10 to 15 hours. Once he got through those he was safe.'

Wilfred Austin Curtis from Havelock, Ontario, was born on 21 August 1893. After a period in the army, then pilot training he flew with 6 Naval Squadron before moving to 10 Naval Squadron on 28 August 1917. Between September 1917 and January 1918 he claimed 13 victories – four destroyed and nine out of control – to win the DSC and Bar. Curtis was later to serve with the RCAF, and in World War 2 he rose to the rank of Air Marshal CB and CBE. He retired in 1953 as Chief of the Canadian Air Staff, and became a director in a number of companies, not least the Hawker Siddeley (Canada) Company. Curtis died on 7 August 1977.

Birmingham-born (on 29 April 1892) Solomon Clifford Joseph joined the RNAS in August 1917. Serving initially with 12 Naval Squadron, he then went to 10 Naval Squadron in February 1918, but it was not until 7 May that he claimed his first German aircraft, an Albatros D V scout. On 6 June Joseph became an ace, and by the end of the war he had achieved 13 victories, including one balloon, and received the DFC and Bar. He had been wounded on 24 September but returned to duty to gain his last victory on 30 October.

Another 13-victory ace in 10 Naval Squadron was John Gerald Manuel from Alberta, born on 29 March 1893. Transferred to the RNAS from the Canadian Field Artillery in March 1917, he had joined 10 Naval Squadron in August. Prior to claiming a kill, Manuel had almost shot himself down on 9 May 1918 whilst using his signal flaregun. The device exploded in flight, blowing out the left side of his cockpit and injuring his hand – after a period in hospital he returned to the front. Manuel's victories, scored between August and June 1918,

won him the DSC and DFC. He was killed in a collision with another pilot on 10 June 1918, aged 25.

Of his 17 victories with 3 and 10 Naval Squadrons, Alfred William 'Nick' Carter accounted for eight with the Camel between February and June 1918. Born in Calgary, Alberta, on 29 April 1894, he joined the RNAS in May 1916 and flew with 3 Wing prior to going to 3 Naval Squadron in April 1917. With five victories on Pups, Carter moved to 10 Naval Squadron and took his score to nine with the Triplane. He won the DSC but was injured in a crash on 11 June. Later, as commander of 'A Flight', Carter forced down two aircraft inside Allied lines. The first of these, on 19 February 1918, was a *Jasta* 3 Albatros D Va whose pilot had been wounded in an engagement with Carter. He wrote in 1966;

'OP of the south bank of the Commines canal by 47th Battalion frontlines at 1153 hrs. I later went up to the frontline in squadron tender and salvaged the rudder from this machine (wrecked) and eventually got it back to Canada. Have it in my Games Room.'

Then on 10 April 1918 he shot down a two-seater LVG of FA 9w inside British lines, its crew also becoming prisoners.

'Low OP and dropping 20-lb bombs in Battle Zone. LVG crashed in flames – I landed in same field but had to leave at once as enemy started shelling, trying to hit my machine.'

Carter subsequently became an instructor, but returned to command No 210 Sqn in the final days of the war. In an interview in 1970, he explained about his first flight in a Camel;

'I remember going out to my new Camel flight and coming under the watchful eyes of its many young pilots, who were looking at this old-timer, with his reputation, and wondering if he could even fly a Camel. I had put it up on a trestle so I could see what the aspect was for take off, for I hadn't flown for at least three months since the summer, and home Canadian leave. No refresher business or anything.

'So I took off, and I kept it right up straight ahead until at about 3000-4000 ft, till I found out what it was all about. Fooled around and got kind of acquainted with it. I tried to do some fast turns and got into a spin right away. However, I learnt (*text continues on page 47*)

This photograph of Camel D3332 (in which Edwin Swale scored four of his last five victories) was taken after the fighter had been taken over by Maj A W 'Nick' Carter in late 1918. He had its markings altered through the addition of his initials *AWC* elaborately painted forward of the fuselage roundel

A W 'Nick' Carter DSC claimed his last eight of seventeen victories with Camels from No 210 Sqn, which he commanded in the final days of the war

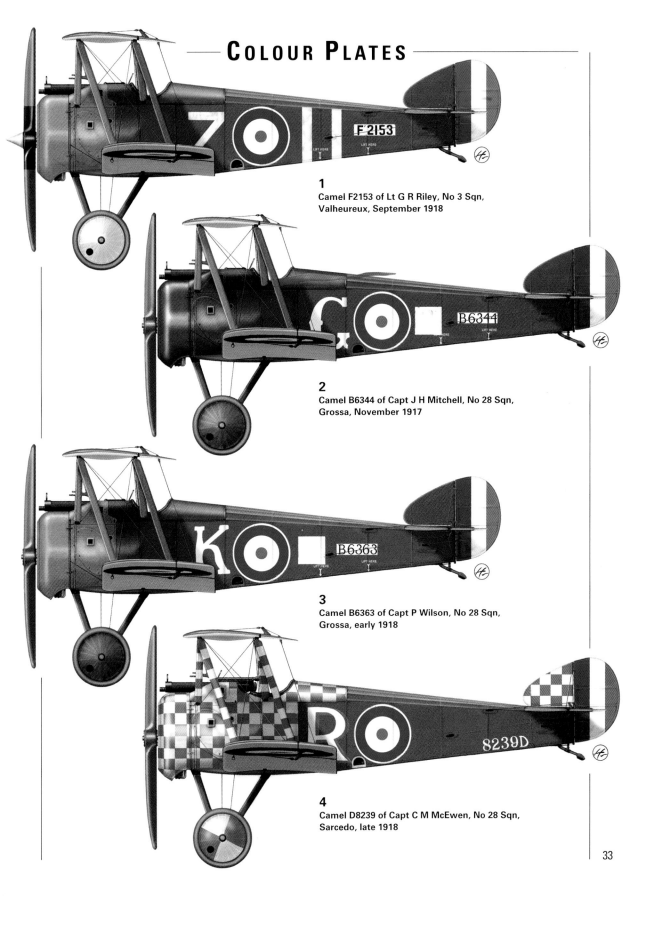

1
Camel F2153 of Lt G R Riley, No 3 Sqn,
Valheureux, September 1918

2
Camel B6344 of Capt J H Mitchell, No 28 Sqn,
Grossa, November 1917

3
Camel B6363 of Capt P Wilson, No 28 Sqn,
Grossa, early 1918

4
Camel D8239 of Capt C M McEwen, No 28 Sqn,
Sarcedo, late 1918

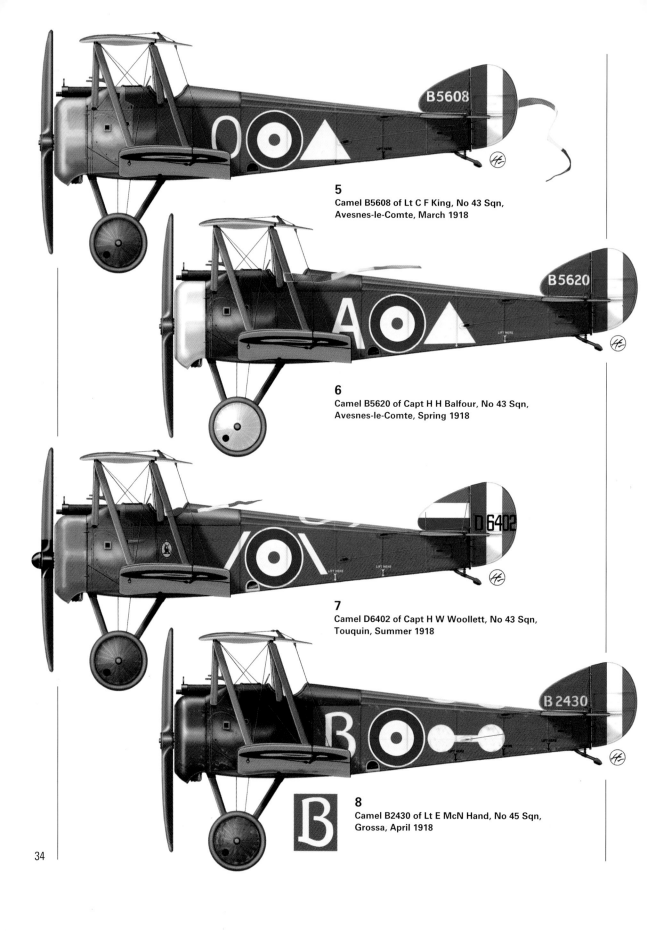

5
Camel B5608 of Lt C F King, No 43 Sqn,
Avesnes-le-Comte, March 1918

6
Camel B5620 of Capt H H Balfour, No 43 Sqn,
Avesnes-le-Comte, Spring 1918

7
Camel D6402 of Capt H W Woollett, No 43 Sqn,
Touquin, Summer 1918

8
Camel B2430 of Lt E McN Hand, No 45 Sqn,
Grossa, April 1918

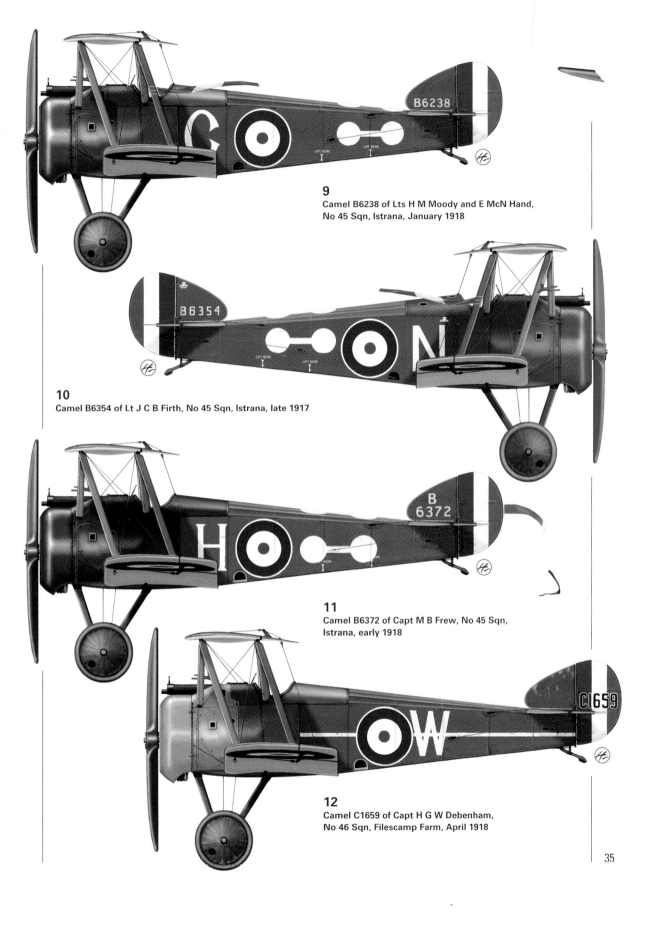

9
Camel B6238 of Lts H M Moody and E McN Hand,
No 45 Sqn, Istrana, January 1918

10
Camel B6354 of Lt J C B Firth, No 45 Sqn, Istrana, late 1917

11
Camel B6372 of Capt M B Frew, No 45 Sqn,
Istrana, early 1918

12
Camel C1659 of Capt H G W Debenham,
No 46 Sqn, Filescamp Farm, April 1918

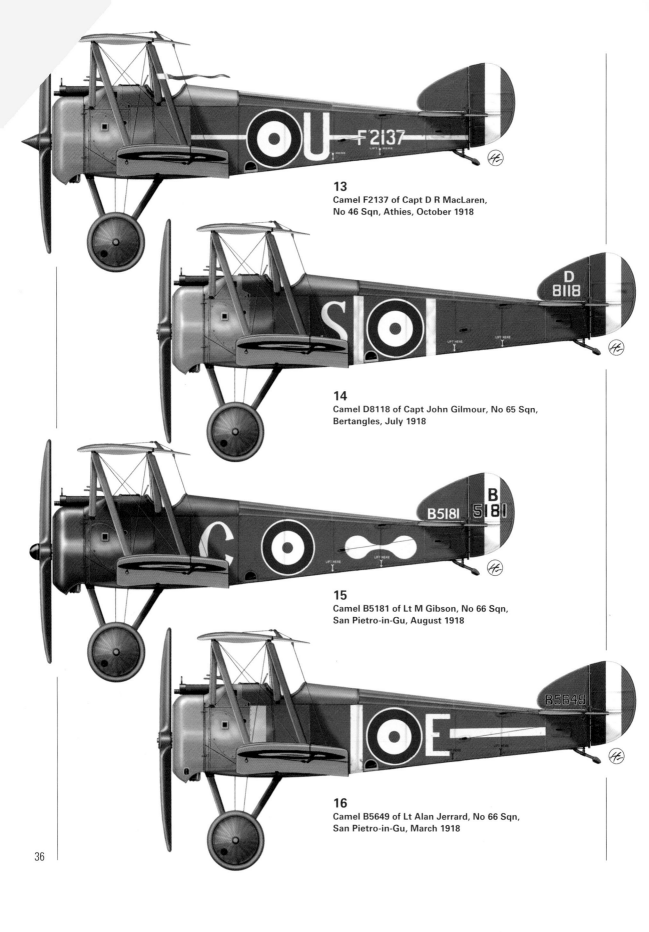

13
Camel F2137 of Capt D R MacLaren,
No 46 Sqn, Athies, October 1918

14
Camel D8118 of Capt John Gilmour, No 65 Sqn,
Bertangles, July 1918

15
Camel B5181 of Lt M Gibson, No 66 Sqn,
San Pietro-in-Gu, August 1918

16
Camel B5649 of Lt Alan Jerrard, No 66 Sqn,
San Pietro-in-Gu, March 1918

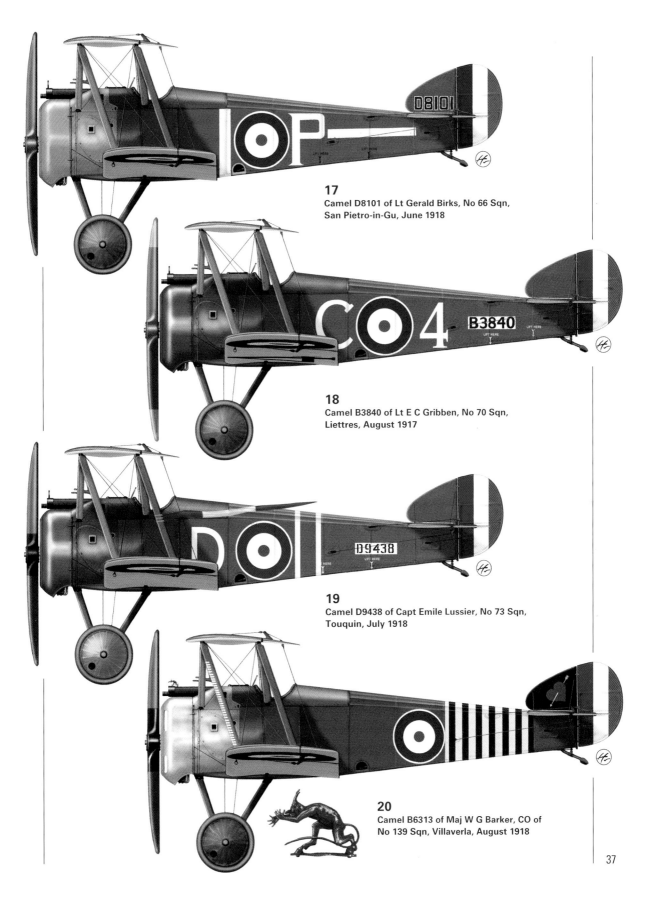

17
Camel D8101 of Lt Gerald Birks, No 66 Sqn,
San Pietro-in-Gu, June 1918

18
Camel B3840 of Lt E C Gribben, No 70 Sqn,
Liettres, August 1917

19
Camel D9438 of Capt Emile Lussier, No 73 Sqn,
Touquin, July 1918

20
Camel B6313 of Maj W G Barker, CO of
No 139 Sqn, Villaverla, August 1918

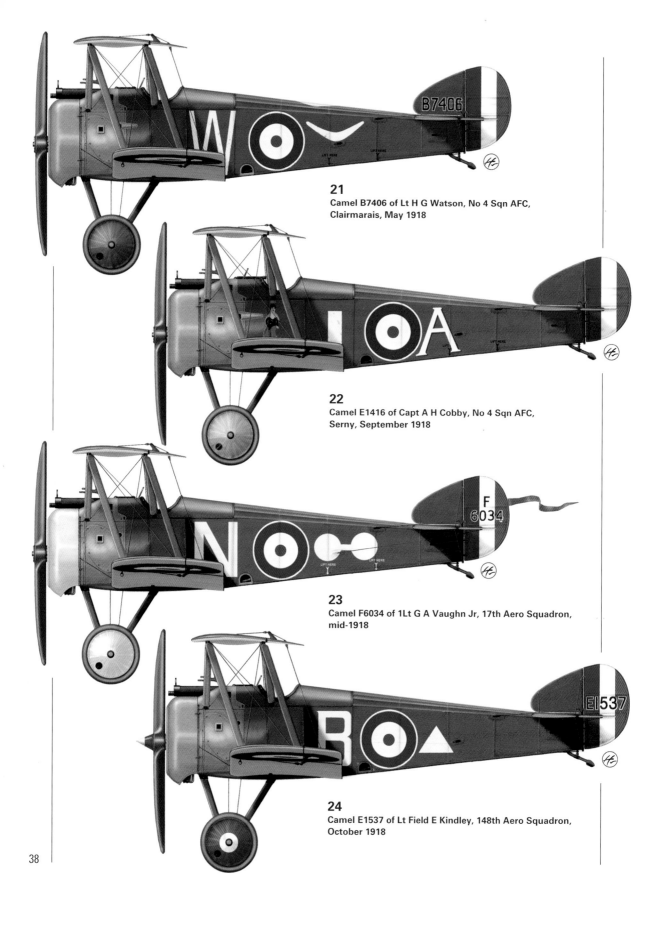

21
Camel B7406 of Lt H G Watson, No 4 Sqn AFC,
Clairmarais, May 1918

22
Camel E1416 of Capt A H Cobby, No 4 Sqn AFC,
Serny, September 1918

23
Camel F6034 of 1Lt G A Vaughn Jr, 17th Aero Squadron,
mid-1918

24
Camel E1537 of Lt Field E Kindley, 148th Aero Squadron,
October 1918

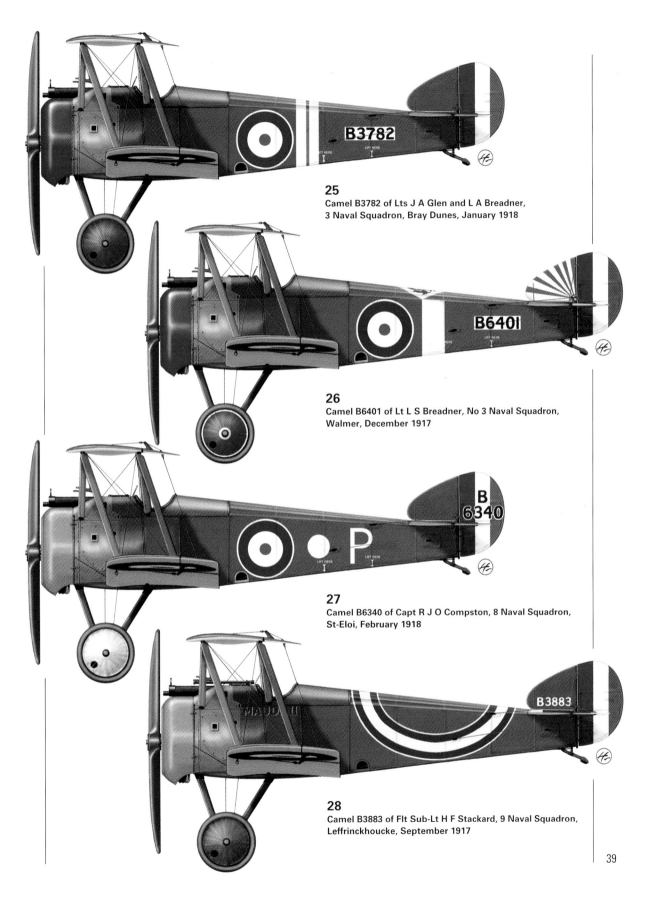

25
Camel B3782 of Lts J A Glen and L A Breadner,
3 Naval Squadron, Bray Dunes, January 1918

26
Camel B6401 of Lt L S Breadner, No 3 Naval Squadron,
Walmer, December 1917

27
Camel B6340 of Capt R J O Compston, 8 Naval Squadron,
St-Eloi, February 1918

28
Camel B3883 of Flt Sub-Lt H F Stackard, 9 Naval Squadron,
Leffrinckhoucke, September 1917

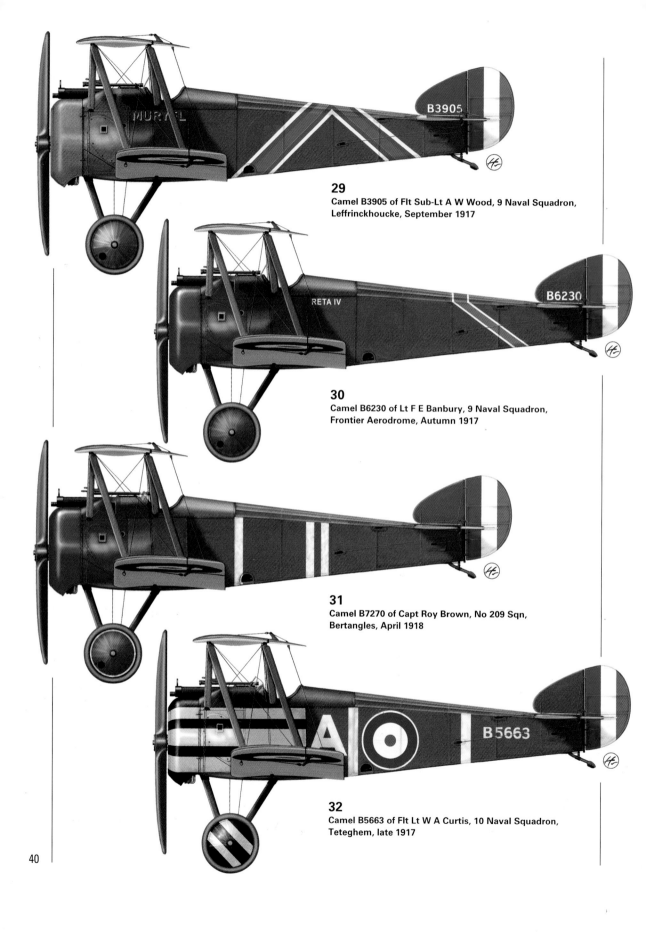

29
Camel B3905 of Flt Sub-Lt A W Wood, 9 Naval Squadron,
Leffrinckhoucke, September 1917

30
Camel B6230 of Lt F E Banbury, 9 Naval Squadron,
Frontier Aerodrome, Autumn 1917

31
Camel B7270 of Capt Roy Brown, No 209 Sqn,
Bertangles, April 1918

32
Camel B5663 of Flt Lt W A Curtis, 10 Naval Squadron,
Teteghem, late 1917

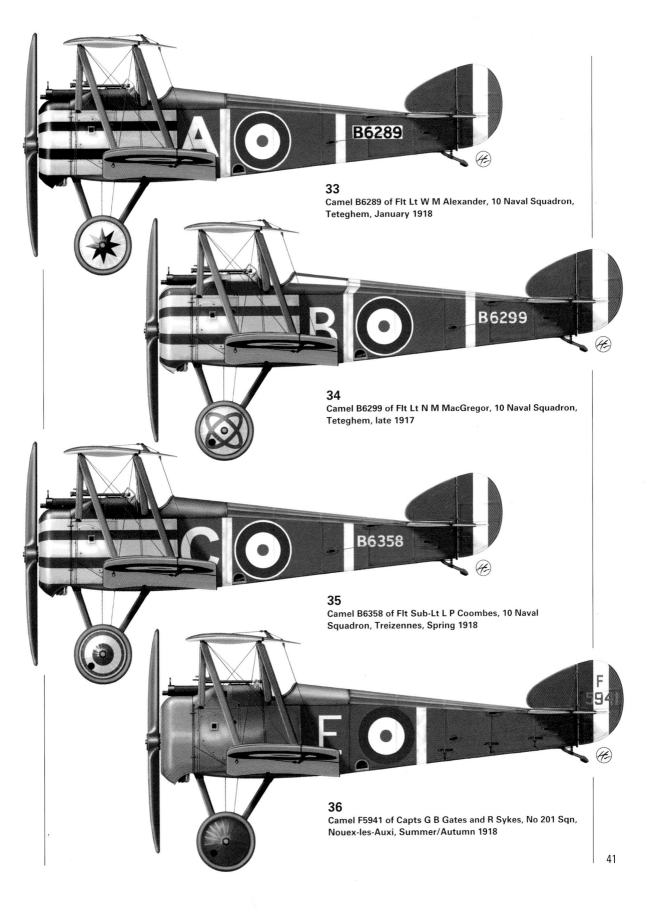

33
Camel B6289 of Flt Lt W M Alexander, 10 Naval Squadron,
Teteghem, January 1918

34
Camel B6299 of Flt Lt N M MacGregor, 10 Naval Squadron,
Teteghem, late 1917

35
Camel B6358 of Flt Sub-Lt L P Coombes, 10 Naval
Squadron, Treizennes, Spring 1918

36
Camel F5941 of Capts G B Gates and R Sykes, No 201 Sqn,
Nouex-les-Auxi, Summer/Autumn 1918

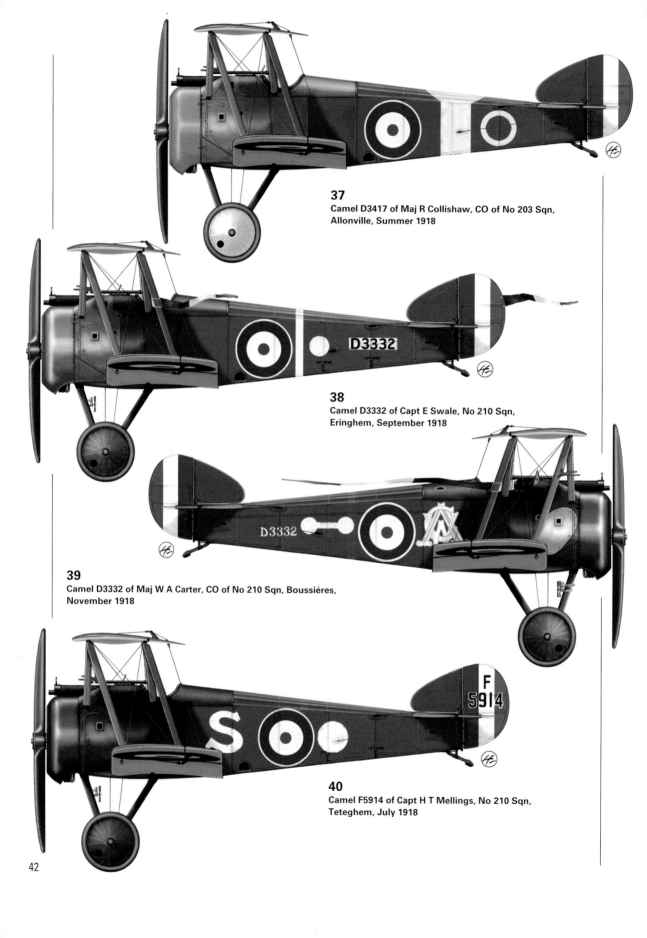

37
Camel D3417 of Maj R Collishaw, CO of No 203 Sqn,
Allonville, Summer 1918

38
Camel D3332 of Capt E Swale, No 210 Sqn,
Eringhem, September 1918

39
Camel D3332 of Maj W A Carter, CO of No 210 Sqn, Boussiéres,
November 1918

40
Camel F5914 of Capt H T Mellings, No 210 Sqn,
Teteghem, July 1918

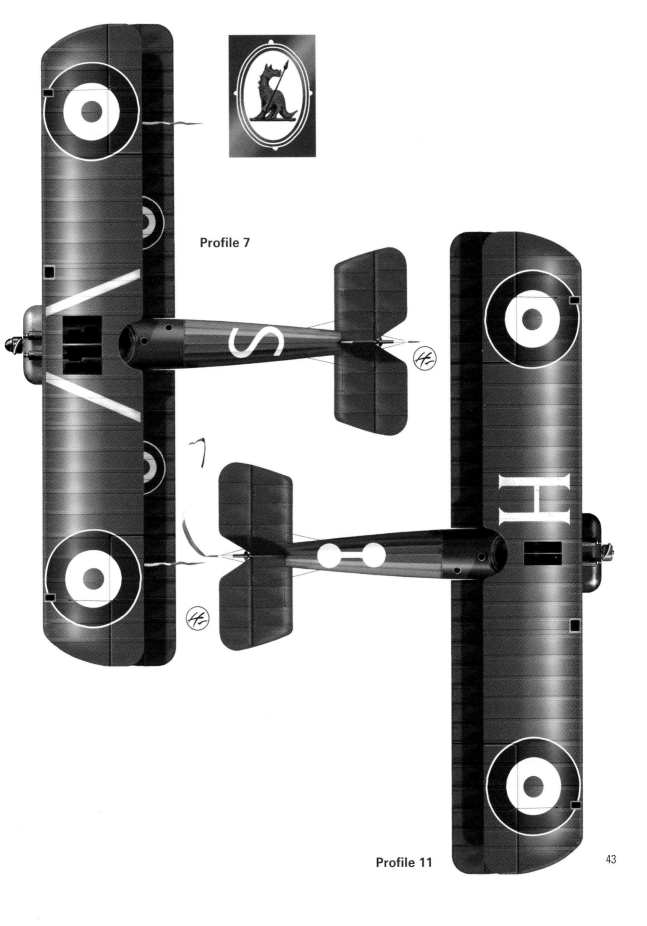

Profile 7

Profile 11

43

Profile 18

Profile 31

Profile 13

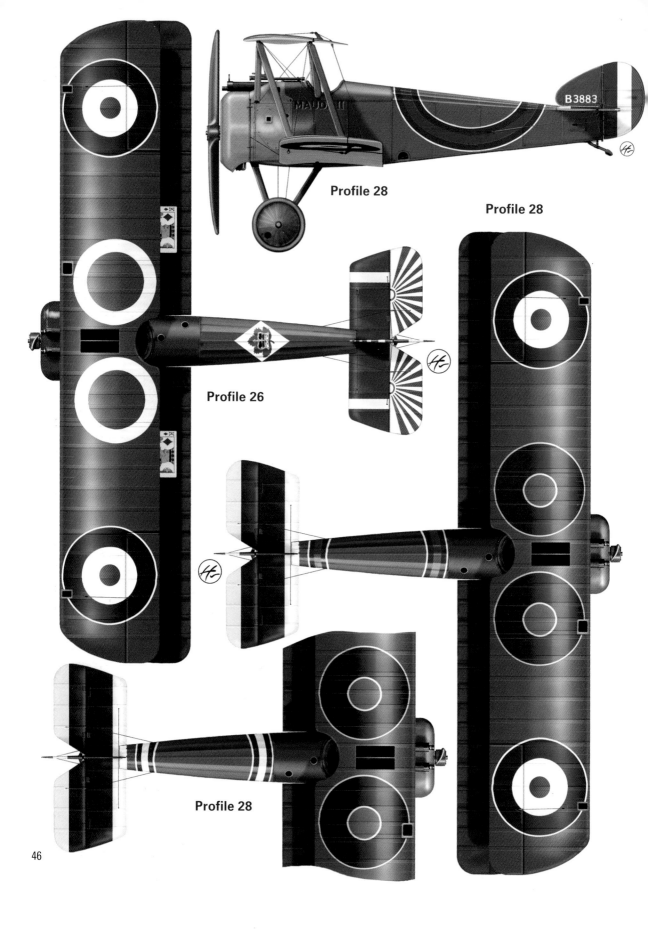

Profile 28

Profile 28

Profile 26

Profile 28

B 3883

MAUD II

46

to fly it. The next day I took the flight on a patrol over the lines and away we went from there.

'The Camel was so sensitive. You had to fly it all the time. When I got used to the aircraft it came easy, and it was wonderful in a dogfight. You could really put it over the Hun in a hurry.'

Carter assisted Ken Unger in destroying a balloon on 1 November 1918 – 'Special Mission, low level to keep balloons down; Lt Unger and I got kite balloon in flames' – and the day before the Armistice he led a ground attack on a German airfield near Binch, east of Mons, in which two two-seaters were destroyed on the ground. 'After the Armistice I went up with my squadron car and found the two machines damaged beyond salvage'.

Carter remained in the RAF and rose to the rank of Air Marshal MBE and OBE. He died in Canada on 17 December 1986.

Another Canadian, from Montreal, William Stanley Jenkins, survived 1918 and gained 12 victories, winning the DFC and Bar in the process. Born on 26 May 1890, he saw action in France with the 87th Canadian Infantry as a corporal, before transferring to the RFC in July 1917. Jenkins was assigned to No 210 Sqn in May 1918 and gained his last two kills on 10 November.

Herbert Andrew Patey came from London, where he was born on 25 September 1898, and initially served in the Royal Naval Division in Egypt and Gallipoli, before being invalided home in September 1915. In November it was discovered that he was under age and he was demobilised. However, Patey joined the RNAS in March 1917. With 10 Naval Squadron by January 1918, he scored his first kill on 17 May, and by 3 September he had claimed 11 victories and won the DFC. Two days later he was himself shot down by Ludwig ('Lutz') Beckmann of *Jasta* 56, becoming the German's eighth and final kill (for Beckmann this was the second No 210 Sqn ace that he had brought down, having killed H T Mellings on 22 July). Patey survived as a PoW, and following the Armistice he arrived home on Christmas Eve. Sadly, he was to die on 18 February 1919, in the massive world 'flu pandemic, still aged only 20.

Two other No 210 Sqn pilots also claimed 11 victories, namely C W Payton and I C Sanderson. Clement Wattson Payton was a Derbyshire man, born on 13 April 1897 and joining the RNAS in November 1917. Arriving at 10 Naval Squadron on the very last day of its pre-RAF existence, his first four claims were made in Camel C62 – Payton's successes gave this aircraft ace status, as another pilot had already scored one victory with it. C62 was involved in the crash on 3 June in which ace Capt W G R Hinchcliffe, was badly injured, losing his left eye. Payton won the DFC but was killed in action on 2 October, his Camel (D9658) being brought down by ground fire whilst he was bombing a train near Courtrai.

Ivan Couper Sanderson was born in Buckinghamshire on 21 December 1899. He joined No 210 Sqn on 9 May 1918, and during the summer of that year claimed 11 victories and won the DFC before being wounded on 17 September.

Harold Thomas Mellings was an experienced aviator. Born in Shropshire on 5 August 1897, he joined the RNAS soon after war

Camels of No 210 Sqn bask in the warm spring sunshine in 1918. Aircraft 'S' (F5914) was usually flown during this period by 15-victory ace Harold T Mellings. Indeed, he was shot down and killed in this machine by Lutz Beckmann of *Jasta* 56 on 22 July 1918

began and saw action with 2 Naval Wing in the eastern Mediterranean from October 1916 through to late 1917. He claimed one victory flying a Bristol Scout and then, using the wing's sole Triplane, he gained at least four more victories, winning the DSC and the Greek War Medal. After a rest period in England, Mellings went to 10 Naval Squadron in January 1918 as a flight commander, and had brought his score to 15 (ten on Camels) by 22 July. As mentioned earlier, Mellings fell to the guns of Lutz Beckmann of *Jasta* 56 on the day he claimed his last victory. By then he had also received a Bar to his DSC, and the DFC had been approved just prior to his death.

Other Camel aces to serve with No 210 Sqn were H B Maund with eight claims during 1917-18, A Buchanan DFC, A L Jones, P Boulton DFC, F V Hall, W R G Hinchcliffe DFC AFC, C F Pineau and G A Welsh, all of whom scored seven kills.

American Archie Buchanan from Long Island, New York, had two claims to fame while with No 210 Sqn apart from his victories. On 17 October 1918 he landed his Camel at Ostend and was informed by the locals that he was the first Allied soldier to enter the town following the Germans departure that morning! However, on 30 October he was shot down by a Fokker D VII flown by Michael Hutterer (his seventh of eight victories) of *Jasta* 23 east of Valenciennes, and he spent the last 12 days prior to the Armistice as a prisoner.

All Percy Boulton's claims were over Fokker biplanes. Hailing from Stoke, he gained his last victory shortly after his 20th birthday. Fred Hall from North London had gained his first victory with 4 Naval Squadron in a Pup, prior to going to 8 Naval Squadron where he was shot down and wounded in May 1917. Assigned to 10 Naval Squadron in October, he was on patrol on 15 May 1918 when an AA shell struck a nearby Camel. The fighter in turn careered into Hall's Camel and he crashed to his death. He too was just 20.

Born on 10 June 1894 in Liverpool, Walter G R Hinchcliffe served in the artillery for the first two years of the war before joining the RNAS. Retained as an instructor at Cranwell, he had notched up 1250 flying hours by the time he finally got back to France. In the first months of 1918 Hinchcliffe scored six victories before a crash on 3 June cost him his left eye. However, his accomplishments thus far brought him the AFC and then the DFC. After the war he flew for KLM Royal Dutch Airlines, and later with Imperial Airways, so his lost eye did not hinder his flying. With over 9000 hours he was one of the most experienced flyers in the world, and in 1928 he planned to fly the Atlantic from east to west with Miss Elsie Mackay, the daughter of Lord Inchcape. They set off on 13 March and were never seen again.

Cleo F Pineau was an American, from Alberquerque, born on 23 July 1893, and he joined the RFC in December 1917. He had enjoyed a varied life up until enlisting, having performed as a clown in a circus, raced as a dirt track rider, then, more soberly, occupied the position of sales manager for Indian Motorcycles in North Carolina. He claimed six Fokker biplanes in the late summer of 1918 and won the DFC, but then got on the wrong end of a Dr I on 8 October and became a prisoner. He died in May 1972 in Williamsport, Pennsylvania, having been President of the Radiant Steel Company in that town.

Norman Miers MacGregor from London (born on 29 May 1896) was yet another Camel ace to fly with 'Naval 10', although he scored his victories with two units. Having learnt to fly in 1916, he scored four kills in the summer of 1917 with 6 Naval Squadron, before moving to 10 Naval Squadron as a flight commander. Here, MacGregor brought his score to seven (possibly eight) by year end. He claimed a Fokker triplane down out of control on 15 September, the aircraft being flown by ace, and leader of *Jasta* 11, Kurt Wolff (33 victories), who fell to his death. Five (possibly six) of his claims were made in B3833, which he flew in both 6 and 10 Naval Squadrons. He received the DSC and in 1918 became an instructor at Eastchurch.

Squadron markings were two vertical white bars which encircled the fuselage, one immediately in front of the fuselage roundel, the other approximately mid-way between this roundel and the tailplane. Flight markings were an 'A', 'B' or 'C' immediately in front of the foremost bar. Unusually, in late 1917 three broad white horizontal bands were painted both on the cowling and aft to a line beneath the rear of the cockpit over a flight colour – black, red or blue – depending on the flight. Individual markings took the form of designs on the wheel covers. However, this was fairly short-lived, and by February 1918 such markings had gone. Flight letters now ceased too, and individual aircraft were denoted by fuselage letter. The following month, the vertical bars were replaced by a white circle aft of the roundel.

13 Naval Squadron/No 213 Sqn

This squadron had unusual beginnings, being formed in Dover in 1915 as a Seaplane flight, using Short 184s and a few French FBA flying-boats. Early in 1916 it was sent to Dunkirk (St Pol) to conduct patrols along the Belgian coast and out into the North Sea, as well as to fly bombing raids on German ports. By 1917 it was equipped with Sopwith Baby and Schneider seaplanes with which it continued its operations and began to combat German Navy aircraft. Because of these actions, Sopwith Pups replaced the seaplanes, and in due course, they too were replaced by Camels in September 1917. Thus the Dunkirk Seaplane Defence Flight (SDF) became a squadron, and eventually was numbered 13 Naval Squadron.

Credited with some 110 victories, it produced 14 aces, the most successful of whom was Capt George Chisholme MacKay, from Toronto, born on 17 May 1898. Joining the RNAS and being posted to the SDF, he began claiming victories soon after 13 Naval Squadron received its first Camels. MacKay remained with the unit until the end of the war, claiming 18 kills during 300+ operational flying hours. Receiving the DFC, CdG and the Belgian Order of Leopold, he returned to Ontario post-war and died on 4 September 1973.

Fellow Canadian John Edmund Greene from Winnipeg (born on 2 July 1894) joined the RNAS in 1916 and began scoring with 13 Naval Squadron in January 1918. He had achieved 15 victories by mid October and had also been awarded the DFC. However, soon after downing victory number 15, on 14 October, Greene was shot down himself, falling in Belgian lines. That day No 213 Sqn lost six Camels to German Marine pilots.

Born on 20 December 1898, Colin Peter Brown came from Sydenham, south-east London, and went to Dulwich College. Joining the RNAS in June 1917, he claim his first victory on 30 November 1917. An aggressive pilot, he attacked land and sea targets as well as combating German aircraft – he once even strafed Zeebrugge harbour at night! In air fighting, Brown accounted for 14 aircraft during 374 combat hours, receiving the DFC and Bar. Remaining in the RAF, he served in Iraq in the late 1920s, and by 1938 was a wing commander, then Senior Air Staff Officer (SASO) 60 Group in 1940-42. He retired as an Air Vice-Marshal CBE and died on 19 October 1965.

After gaining one victory with 9 Naval Squadron in October 1917, John de Campbourne Paynter moved to 10 and then 13 Naval Squadrons. A Hampshire lad, born on 17 May 1898, he had also seen service with 6 Naval Squadron, but it was with 13 Naval Squadron/ No 213 Sqn that he found his touch, and on 1 June 1918 claimed his tenth victory. By then Paynter had received the DSC and been wounded twice. On the night of 18 June the squadron's airfield at Bergues was raided by German bombers and he was fatally wounded by bomb fragments, having refused to take shelter.

John William Pinder claimed victories with three squadrons, firstly three (two on Triplanes) with 9 Naval Squadron in 1917, three with 13 Naval Squadron and six more once it had become No 213 Sqn, and finally five with No 45 Sqn RAF in the final weeks of the war. Of his 17 victories, 15 were with the Camel. Pinder came from Deal, Kent, born on 14 February 1898, and he won the DFC, to which he added a Bar as a flight commander with No 45 Sqn on its return from Italy.

Other aces to serve with 13 Naval Squadron/No 213 Sqn were C J Sims DFC with nine kills, M L Cooper DFC, G S Hodson and D S Ingalls with six and M J G Day, W E Gray, H C Smith and A H Turner with five. Charles Sims scored a unique double in one combat when he shot down a Fokker D VII which spun into another. He and Maurice Cooper both came from Bournemouth, although the latter was born in Dublin. Cooper did not survive the war, being brought down by ground fire during an attack on a train on 2 October 1918.

George Stanley Hodson was a ten-victory Camel ace, his first four claims coming whilst serving with No 73 Sqn RAF in March 1918.

Colin Brown DFC and Bar was credited with 14 kills whilst flying with 13 Naval Squadron/No 213 Sqn between November 1917 and war's end

Born on 2 May 1899 in Belmont, Surrey, he was another Dulwich College ace. Joining No 213 Sqn in September, Hodson's tenth kill went down on 14 October, and although he was recommended for the DFC, it was not approved. Remaining in the RAF, he became an Air Marshal CB CBE AFC, having served with the RNZAF on exchange between 1938-43. Hodson was AOC Coastal Command post-war, and later SASO Home Command. He died on 1 October 1976.

American David Ingalls was the only US Navy ace of World War 1. Hailing from Cleveland, Ohio, he was only 19 when he went into action in the summer of 1918, claiming six combat victories whilst attached to No 213 Sqn. He had earlier served with a coastal patrol unit but found this dull, so he flew Camels with the RAF until made to fly DH 4 bombers, although he eventually managed a posting back to No 213 Sqn. Ingalls won the DFC and an American DSC. Post-war he became a lawyer, but served again in World War 2 as a Navy commander, retiring as a rear-admiral in the naval reserve. Later a vice-president of Pan Am Airways, Ingalls died on 26 April 1985.

Ex-RNAS test pilot Miles Day DSC was killed in action off Dunkirk on 27 February 1918. William Gray from Berwick on Tweed also received a DFC for his five victories in 1918.

An interesting Camel ace who scored four victories with SDF, 13 Naval Squadron and No 213 Sqn was Leonard Horatio Slatter, born on 8 December 1894 in Durban, South Africa. When war came he was a despatch rider with the Navy's armoured cars, then he became an observer with the RNAS. Once a pilot, Slatter flew Pups with the SDF, claiming two victories, then came his four Camel claims with 13 Naval Squadron/No 213 Sqn. His fifth Camel victory (and his seventh overall) came on 30 August 1918 while with No 4 ASD. This won him the DFC, which he added to his previous DSC and Bar.

Slatter remained in the RAF post-war, serving in South Russia (and being awarded an OBE) and eventually attaining the rank of Air Marshal. His long career included a period as CO of the RAF's High Speed Flight in 1926-27, and captain of the Schneider Trophy Team in Venice. After a solo flight from England to South Africa in 1929, he commanded Nos 19, 111 and 43 Sqns in England in the 1930s. Slatter was also SASO aboard HMS *Courageous* in 1932-35. During World War 2 he commanded Coastal Command's 15 Group, and in 1945 became AOC-in-C of this command. He died on 14 April 1961.

13 Naval Squadron's Camel markings consisted of coloured stripes, or bands, painted diagonally across the fuselage, and individual letters in lieu of fuselage roundels to denote the pilot. Once it became No 213 Sqn, there appears to have been no unit marking adopted, and any decoration that appeared was seemingly at the whim of the pilot.

Displaying a mix of well worn Navy and RFC uniforms, pilots of No 213 Sqn pose for the camera along with the near obligatory mascot. Second from the left is W E Gray DFC (five victories), while 4th from the left is J W Pinder DFC and Bar (17 victories, of which 15 were on Camels with 9 Naval Squadron, 13 Naval Squadron/No 213 Sqn and No 45 Sqn) (*Bruce/Leslie collection*)

David Ingalls DFC DSC(US) (centre) of No 213 Sqn was the sole US Navy ace of World War 1. Standing to his left is Ken McLeish US Navy, who was killed in action on 14 October 1918. The other pilot is Edward 'Shorty' Smith US Navy. 14 October was a bad day for No 213 Sqn, as six of its pilots were killed (*Bruce/Leslie collection*)

RFC AND RAF CAMEL ACES

I t quickly became apparent to the RFC that the Sopwith Camel was fairly well suited to ground attack operations. For one thing, its cockpit was further forward than its great rival the SE 5a, giving the pilot a better view of the ground at low level, and its turning ability gave it that edge if challenged by ground fire. Not that SE 5as, or any other aircraft, were not used for ground attack sorties, but more commonly they were used in times of extreme urgency.

The first real test for the Camel in this new role came during the Cambrai offensive of November 1917. No 46 Sqn had only just swapped its Pups for the Camel when the Cambrai battle began – famous for the use of tanks for the first time on a massive scale. No 46 Sqn was one of a number of units briefed to support the tanks by attacking ground targets, including gun positions, as well as bombing nearby German airfields. Arthur Gould Lee was in the squadron at the time, and recalled well when I met him in the late 1960s the dangers of low flying, especially in foggy, misty conditions when pilots could find themselves over the frontline, amidst a shower of rifle and machine gun fire, before they realised what was happening. He once recorded;

'We ran into mist and low cloud as soon as we took off, and as we were flying at 50 ft, we were much too occupied in keeping the compass steady to check our route on the map. Suddenly, there was a tremendous racket of gun fire from below, and bullets cracked past our ears. My faulty compass had led us bang across the lines at Bullecourt. We slithered hastily around and fled westwards.'

Lee also wrote about formation flying with the Camel;

'I found it tiring to fly in formation for a long patrol. She's so sensitive you can't relax for a second, and you have the constant pressure on the joystick, which in two hours' flying makes your right arm ache. But she's such a marvellous aeroplane that these handicaps are unimportant. But imagine after waiting all those months for Camels, striving not to be shot down on Pups, and looking forward to toppling Huns two at a time with my two Vickers, to find myself switched to ground strafing!'

And his thought during an actual ground attack sortie;

'In this blind confusion there wasn't a hope of picking and choosing. The main thing was to get rid of the darned bombs before a bullet hit them. In a sharp turn I saw a bunch of guns right in line for attack, so dived at 45 degrees and released all four bombs. As I swung aside I saw them burst, a group of white-grey puffs centred with red flames – one bomb between two guns, the rest a few yards away.

'Splinters suddenly splash my face – a bullet through a centre-section strut. This makes me go hot, and I dive at another group of guns, giving them 100 rounds. I see a machine gun blazing at me so I swing on to that, and one short burst and he stops firing. As I climb up, a Camel whizzes past me out of the mist, missing me by a yard. It makes me sweat with fright. This is too dangerous, and I lift into the cloud to 300 ft, stay there half a minute, then come down. Lateau Wood is behind me. There isn't much room below, and I nearly hit a high tree. Swerving violently, I skim through tree-tops with the mist clinging to the branches, then suddenly no trees, an open road. I fly along it trying to get my breath.

'Then suddenly "rak-ak-ak-ak!" and tracer! I swung the Camel violently around. Two V-strutters (Albatros Scouts) were coming up behind me, guns flashing, a third behind them.

'I was in no frame of mind for heroic air combat at 300 ft, but to save my skin I swung sharply round again. I put a burst into the first Hun as he whizzed past me, did another right turn, and fired another burst at the second Hun and then my guns jammed.

'There was only one thing to do, and I did it – climb up into the clouds. I'd never flown a Camel for any length of time in cloud, and I found it tricky. The tail-heavy feeling, the need for constant pressure on the stick, the tendency to swing left and to spin. Meanwhile, I cleared my guns.'

Coming out of cloud and uncertain of his position, Lee suddenly saw German cavalry ahead of him.

'I swung over, dived, and let them have it. Some horses and men tumbled, the rest scattered. I went on to the sunken road they'd come from. It was full of horsed traffic. I dived on them and let them have it too, and saw men falling off stampeding horses. My dive carried me on to another road, with a column of marching troops. As I fired they bumped into another one, then broke into the side fields. Scores rushed into a thicket. I flew at it level at 20 ft and gave them 100 rounds. Surely one or two found a billet!'

There is no doubt that these aerial attacks inflicted significant casualties on German troops, and surely demoralised them. It was a tactic, once learnt, that the RFC and RAF used to great effect for the remainder of the war, and the Camel was in the forefront of such sorties. Aircraft of all types took part in such operations during the Germans' March Offensive in 1918, and one only has to read Victor Yeates' book *Winged Victory* (a novel, but based on his experiences with No 46 Sqn) to understand the RFC's low level missions. Laurence Coombes of No 210 Sqn, whom we met earlier, wrote of the following April battles;

'The Germans began another big offensive early in April near Ypres, near to where we were. The Portuguese held the line near Ypres and gave up when the Germans attacked, retreating in disorder. A big salient formed at this point of weakness, and the front was in such a state of flux that nobody knew where it was, and one had to be careful to distinguish friend from foe when ground strafing. The weather was bad around 8 April – low cloud and mist – so we were sent to ground strafe and drop 20-lb bombs on any targets we could find.

'On 11 April I was on another low bombing patrol. After dropping bombs on some barges and firing at transport vehicles, I was flying at

300 ft when I was shot up from the ground. The engine stopped and I prepared to force-land when I felt petrol soaking the seat of my pants. I realised that the main pressure tank on which the pilot sat was holed, so I switched to the gravity tank and the engine picked up. When I got back it was found that besides the petrol tank, two cylinders had been pierced – it was a miracle the engine kept going.'

John Summers of No 209 Sqn also related to me his experiences of a ground attack sortie during the August 1918 offensive;

'Soon after midday on 8 August 1918 – the first day of the big push – I was flying Camel B7471, accompanied by Capt Drake in another Camel from my flight. We found a number of our cavalry whose advance was being held up by a large party of enemy troops defending a sunken crossroads. I dropped my four bombs from 150 ft – three hit the road and the other the active building at the crossroads. I doubt if the three did much damage, but Drake, coming behind, dropped all his right in the middle of the sunken road, killing many of the defenders. We then attacked with our machine guns and the remainder fled. We drove them right through the village behind the crossroads, flew up and down the streets at chimney height without drawing any fire, and then went and waved to our cavalry who collected their horses and occupied the village without further opposition.

'Those first four days of the battle were pretty hectic and we suffered quite a few casualties both in men and machines. I had to exchange my machine four times in four days.'

Camel B7471 gained five victories for its pilots (including three aces) in Nos 70 and 209 Sqns before being lost on 12 August 1918.

No 3 Sqn

This unit had earlier been used for Army cooperation missions – artillery spotting and reconnaissance – flying Bristol Scouts, Moranes and BE 2s. Then, in October 1917, it became a fighter outfit with the arrival of the Camel. Aside from flying many ground attack sorties. No 3 Sqn's pilot claimed 120 kills, and nine aces were produced.

The squadron's leading ace was Capt Douglas John Bell from South Africa, who was born on 16 September 1893. He joined the RFC in June 1916 and his first unit was No 27 Sqn, arriving in October. Bell scored three victories with this mainly bomber unit, and after a period in England on Home Defence duties, became a flight commander with No 3 Sqn in February 1918. During that hectic March/April period Bell accounted for 17 German aircraft and balloons before he was shot down attacking a two-seater on 27 May and killed. He was flying C6730, in which he had scored seven of his victories – his previous Camel had been C1615, with which he had scored his previous ten kills. C1615 had been lost on 24 March, downed by ground fire during an attack on German positions. Bell had won the MC and Bar.

Born on 23 February 1899, Londoner George Raby Riley joined No 3 Sqn on his 18th birthday. Within a month he had scored his first victory, and by late September had run his score to 13 to win the MC and DFC. Following his fourth victory, Riley was wounded on

South African Capt D J Bell MC and Bar was the ranking ace of No 3 Sqn, scoring 17 (of his 20) victories with the unit in Camels. Serving with a variety of frontline squadrons from October 1916, Douglas Bell was eventually shot down and killed in No 3 Sqn Camel C6730 by the gunner of a German two-seater on 27 May 1918

20 April 1918, but returned to the unit and 'made ace' on 8 August. Five of his claims were against balloons – highly dangerous targets.

Will Hubbard, from Leamington Spa, claimed his tenth and No 3 Sqn's last victory on 29 October 1918. Born on 25 February 1895, he became a flight commander with No 3 Sqn, and his first three victims were DFW two-seaters, two of which he despatched on 14 May 1918. Hubbard almost became a prisoner on 26 August, being forced to land inside German territory with engine failure. While trying to fix his Camel, a German soldier shot at him, holing his fighter's fuel tank, but he managed to get the engine going and just had sufficient fuel left to get across the trenches, where he crash-landed.

Other No 3 Sqn aces were A W Franklyn and H L Wallace with six and L A Hamilton, D J Hughes, W H Maxted and N R Smuts with five. Adrian W Franklyn, from Hounslow, became 19 the day the RAF was formed, by which time he was already with No 3 Sqn in France. His first three victories won for him the MC, and he remained in the RAF post-war, retiring as a group captain in 1948.

Hazel LeRoy Wallace was a Canadian, born on 13 November 1897, and was already a Camel ace when he joined No 3 Sqn. Having entered the RNAS in October 1916, his first two units had been 9 Naval Squadron (two victories) and then 1 Naval Squadron/No 201 Sqn (six victories). Wallace's six kills with No 3 Sqn resulted in him receiving the DFC. He and his flight also destroyed three aircraft on the ground and burnt a hangar. Wallace died on 22 March 1976.

New Yorker Lloyd A Hamilton became an ace with the No 3 Sqn in the spring of 1918, and doubled his score as a flight commander with the US 17th Aero Squadron in August before his death in action on 24 August. David J Hughes, a Welshman, won the DFC for his five kills, scored in the last months of the war, including a Fokker D VII from *Jasta* 79b which he forced down inside Allied lines on 4 September.

William H Maxted survived the last months of the war, shooting down two Fokkers, two LVGs and a balloon, only to be killed on 17 December 1918. Diving on a ground target during flight practice, his Camel (H809) broke up in the air. All five of his victories had been scored in B7905. Finally, five-kill ace Neil Smuts, as his name might suggest, came from South Africa. He had won the DFC and become a flight commander all before his 20th birthday.

No 43 Sqn

Formed in April 1916, this unit first went to France in early 1917 with Sopwith two-seaters, which were replaced by Camels in September 1917. One year later it was one of only two squadrons in France to operate with the Sopwith Snipe. By war's end its pilots had claimed 122 victories, and ten aces had been produced.

Henry Winslow Woollett from Suffolk, born on 5 August 1895, was No 43 Sqn's leading light. A doctor's son, he served as a second lieutenant in the Lincolnshire Regiment when war came and saw action in the Dardanelles. Woollett transferred to the RFC in June 1916, and his first unit was No 24 Sqn, flying DH 2 'pushers' and

Londoner A W Franklyn MC of No 3 Sqn was just 19 when he claimed his six victories during the course of 1918. Remaining in the RAF post-war, he retired with the rank of group captain in 1948

Henry Woollett DSO MC and Bar of No 43 Sqn poses in his Camel D6402, which he had marked with the green dragon motif seen immediately below the cockpit. Some 30 of his 35 victories were scored in Camels (23 in this machine alone), including 11 balloons

Woollett's D6402 heads a line up of No 43 Sqn Camels in France in the summer of 1918. At one stage this long-lived fighter featured the letter 'S' on the fuselage, along with the unit's white triangle and two white bands. To these markings Woollett then added white blotches in the hope that they would help camouflage his aircraft during his balloon assaults (*via Mike O'Connor*)

then DH 5s with their back-staggered top wings. He claimed five victories with this unit in 1917, won the MC and then returned to England. In March 1918 Woollett returned to France as a flight commander with No 43 Sqn and had claimed a further 30 kills by early August.

With a Bar to his MC, the DSO and the French *Légion d'Honneur* and CdG, and twice Mentioned in Despatches, Woollett was posted back to England to command a training wing. In the peacetime RAF he served in Iraq and led No 23 Sqn in England in the early 1930s. He died on 31 October 1969. Among his victories were 11 balloons, and on 12 April 1918 he claimed six German aircraft in two engagements. No fewer than 23 of Woollett's Camel claims came in D6402, which he eventually overturned and damaged after landing on 21 July.

A second pilot in No 43 Sqn claimed six victories in one day – John Lightfoot Trollope from Wallington (born on 30 May 1897). A despatch rider prior to joining the RFC, he had flown Sopwith 1½ Strutters with No 70 Sqn prior to being a single-seat pilot. Once with No 43 Sqn in late 1917, he began scoring in the new year, and in March accounted for 15 of his 18 victories, including six and one shared on the 24th, and three more on the 28th. However, during this latter action he was himself brought down by ace Paul Billik of *Jasta* 52, so his final three victories were reported in his absence. Badly wounded in the left hand, Trollope was taken prisoner and eventually had to have his whole arm amputated at the shoulder. He received the MC and Bar after his capture. In World War 2 Trollope served as a wing commander between 1940-43 in Maintenance Command.

Cecil Frederick King scored 22 victories with No 43 Sqn, three of them in Snipes at the end of the war. From Kent, but living in Chelmsford when war came, he had been born on 19 February 1899. A private in the Essex Regiment OTC, he joined the RFC in February 1917 and served with No 43 Sqn from the autumn of 1917. He won the MC just prior to being slightly wounded on 28 March in the same fight in which John Trollope was lost. Within days King was

commanding Trollope's old flight, and his further victories won for him the DFC and CdG. King was killed in a flying accident on 24 January 1919.

A Welshman from Llandudno, Charles Chaplin 'Sandy' Banks had been a school teacher pre-war. After serving with the 5th Battalion of the Royal Welsh Fusiliers he became a Camel pilot, and his first success was a Gotha G V bomber while flying with No 44 Home Defence Sqn in England. He shared this with Capt G H Hackwill, a future Camel ace with No 54 Sqn. The G V, from *Bogohl* 3, fell in flames at 2210 hrs near Wickford, thus becoming the first Gotha bomber to be brought down at night over England. Both Banks and Hackwill received the MC for their efforts, the former having earlier received a Mention in Despatches in December 1917 for his nightfighting exploits.

In early February Banks went to France to become a flight commander with No 43 Sqn, winning the DFC and scoring nine further Camel victories before the arrival of the Snipe. Flying the latter type, he downed a further three Fokker D VIIs in the final weeks of the war, bringing his score to 13. The Gotha was not his only night kill, for on 31 May he had brought down a huge Friedrichshafen bomber over France for his seventh victory. Banks had had a break from combat between July and September 1918, working as an instructor at No 4 Flying School. He left the RAF in January 1919. Banks's son was a fighter pilot in World War 2 in Italy, and he was shot down and fought with the partisans until finally being captured and executed.

Other Camel aces of No 43 Sqn were H H Balfour MC, H C Daniel MC AFC, G C Bailey DFC, R J Owen and G A Lingham. Capt Harold Balfour gained nine victories, seven on Camels. He was later an MP and became Under-Secretary of State for Air and a Minister for Aviation pre-World War 2. He became Lord Balfour of Inchrye and died in September 1988.

Hector Cyril 'Daisy' Daniel came from South Africa, his nine victories being scored between February and May 1918, whence he became an instructor, gaining the AFC. Serving with the South African Air Force post-war, he had risen to the rank of lieutenant-colonel by 1939, and later brigadier, as SASO SAAF during the East African Campaign. Sadly, Daniel subsequently took his own life shortly after World War 2.

Born on 10 March 1899, Geoffrey 'Lumpy' Bailey scored eight victories, his first being scored on 16 February 1918. Robert Owen was credited with his seventh victory on 28 March 1918 in the same engagement in which he was later brought down and taken prisoner. He did not claim the kill himself, but Capt Trollope did upon his early release from captivity.

No 43 Sqn's John Trollope MC and Bar scored 18 victories, including six on 24 March 1918. Four days later he was shot down by German ace Paul Billik of *Jasta* 52, suffering a serious hand wound in the process. Made a PoW, Trollope later had to have his whole left arm amputated at the shoulder as a result of this injury

Australian G A 'Flossy' Lingham DFC claimed six kills with No 43 Sqn in 1918

One of the most successful Camel aces of the war, Canadian Capt Donald MacLaren DSO MC and Bar DFC was credited with no fewer than 54 victories between March and October 1918. Flying exclusively with No 46 Sqn, he survived the war and eventually passed away in July 1989 at the ripe old age of 96 (*Mike O'Connor*)

Hailing from Melbourne, Australia, George 'Flossy' Lingham collected a DFC for his six victories. He went into civil aviation post-war and in the 1930s was a Director of the Heston Aircraft Company.

No 46 Sqn

Formed in April 1916, this unit was yet another which began life flying two-seaters, in this case Nieuports. Early in 1917 these were exchanged for Pups and then in July No 46 Sqn enjoyed a break in England on Home Defence duties. Returning to France, the squadron received Camels in November. Apart from air fighting patrols, No 46 Sqn also flew ground attack sorties. By the Armistice the unit had achieved 184 victories, and 16 aces had been created.

The squadron, like several of its contemporaries, was keen on shared victories, and this fact was reflected in the scores of many of its pilots.

No 46 Sqn's leading ace was Canadian Donald Roderick MacLaren. Born in Ottawa on 28 May 1893, he moved with his family to Calgary, and as a boy became an expert marksman with a rifle. Poor health prevented an immediate entry into military service, but in May 1917 MacLaren joined the RFC and became a flight instructor in Ontario. Finally getting to France in November, he was assigned to No 46 Sqn. A slow starter, his first claim came on 6 March 1918, but by the end of that month, covering the German March offensive, his score had reached 13, and by the end of May it had progressed to an amazing 32. June was a bad month for MacLaren, bringing just two kills, but July saw seven, and August four more. Seven in September and two more in early October brought his tally to 54, 16 of which had been shared.

MacLaren's first run of successes (19 kills) came in Camel B9153, then D6418 (18 kills). Eight victories in D6603 and his final nine in F2137 gave him his 54 claims in just four aircraft! His rewards were the DSO, MC and Bar, DFC and the French *Légion d'Honneur* and CdG. A broken leg on 10 October 1918 ended his war flying, and as a major MacLaren later helped in forming the RCAF, but soon afterwards went into commercial aviation. He died in July 1989.

The second-ranking Camel ace in No 46 Sqn was George Edwin Thomson from Dumbarton, Scotland, born on 19 September 1897. Pre-war, he had spent time in Rangoon with his family, but returned to join the colours. After service with the King's Own Scottish Borderers, Thomson went into the RFC in September 1916. He flew Pups with No 46 Sqn, gaining one victory, then added a further 20 on Camels by 23 March 1918. Returning to England as an instructor, with the DSO and MC, he was killed at Port Meadow, Oxford, on 23 May 1918 whilst flying with No 7 Training Depot Station (TDS). Soon after take-off, Thomson's aircraft burst into flames and he was killed when it crashed.

Other No 46 Sqn Camel aces were C J Marchant MC with at least nine kills, H N C Robinson MC, J H Smith and A G Vlasto with eight apiece, R K McConnell DFC and C W Odell with seven (Odell had two on Pups and five on Camels), M M Freehill DFC, C H Sawyer, P M Tudhope DFC each with six, and H G W Debenham and V M Yeates with five.

Cecil 'Chips' Marchant, from London, first served in the trenches aged 18, but eventually joined the RFC and flew Pups and Camels with No 46 Sqn. His nine victories were scored between March and May 1918 while a flight commander. A wound put Marchant out of the war, and post-war he went into the family business until his death in the 1960s. Eight (possibly nine) of his claims were made in Camel B9211.

Harry Robinson flew Pups and Camels with No 46 Sqn from late 1917 through to April 1918, at which time he moved to No 70 Sqn as a flight commander. Whilst with the latter unit he added two more victories to bring his score to ten. On one occasion Robinson was forced to break off a patrol due to poor fuel pressure, and on his way back home he spotted seven German aircraft attacking a British two-seater. Despite his problem, he engaged them and drove off the enemy, claiming one destroyed before his guns jammed. To his MC Robinson later added the CdG and, post-war, the DFC for operations in Mesopotamia in 1921.

Donald MacLaren used F2137 'U' to claim his last nine kills in September-October 1918. Its pointed nose spinner was painted red, and a black 'U' appeared under the starboard lower wing (note the same marking applied to Camel 'S' in the background). Its wheel covers may have also been painted red as a flight marking

This view of Donald MacLaren and his Camel reveals the white line that ran down the top decking of the fighter's fuselage. The two darker lines are red in colour, as are the two wing strut pennants. Not explained is why there appears to be the letter 'G' on the upper starboard wing just inboard of the centre section, unless this is an earlier aircraft so marked

Maurice Freehill added a seventh victory to his No 46 Sqn total when he downed a Fokker D VII while serving as a flight commander with No 80 Sqn in October 1918. On 4 November he knocked out a German machine-gun position which was holding up British troops, and later, during a low-level recce mission, Freehill brought back valuable intelligence despite intense ground fire. He remained in the RAF after the war.

Essex-born Horace Debenham also scored a victory – his sixth – with another unit, namely No 208 Sqn, in May 1918, where he

Essex-born Capt H G W Debenham of No 46 Sqn claimed four of his six victories in C1659 in early 1918

Lt Alexander G Vlasto of No 46 Sqn was credited with eight victories. He succumbed to TB in the 1930s

served as a flight commander. He had previously claimed his first five victories with No 46 Sqn in the opening weeks of 1918, Debenham having initially served as an observer in the squadron prior to receiving pilot training.

Victor Maslin Yeates gained fame in the final years of his life thanks to his novel *Winged Victory* which, as mentioned earlier in this chapter, was based on his experiences with No 46 Sqn. He claimed five victories with the unit between May and August 1918, and flew numerous ground attack sorties. However, these missions took a toll on his health, and Yeates died of TB in December 1934, as did his squadronmate, and eight-kill ace, Alexander Vlasto, during the same decade.

No 54 Sqn

This squadron was another ex-Pup unit, formed originally in May 1916, and taking its machines to France in December. Over 50 German aircraft had been claimed by the time the Camel arrived a year later, and No 54 Sqn undertook much ground attack work in the last year of the war. Capt H H Maddocks MC, who had four Pup victories, scored the unit's first Camel success (in B9143) on 3 January 1918, 'flaming' a DFW to give him ace status;

'Enemy Aircraft (EA) was seen crossing the lines north of St Quentin at 0825 hrs. Capt Maddocks dived and got under his tail. After a short burst EA was seen to catch fire and go down south of St Quentin.'

His next two 'flamers' were Albatros Scouts of *Jasta* 48, which he claimed on 3 February.

No 54 Sqn had added a further 80+ victories to its Pup tally by war's end, but its losses were heavy. In fact 40 Camels were lost between February and April 1918 alone. The unit did not produce any high-scoring aces, although 11 of its pilots claimed five or more victories, with the highest, Canadian Ernest James Salter from Greenbank, Ontario (born on 9 November 1897) downing nine aircraft. Between June and August he destroyed five two-seaters and four scouts, and was then wounded on 2 September. Salter's reward for his efforts came from the French, who made him a Chevalier of the *Légion d'Honneur*, and presented him with the CdG with Palme. He died on 23 March 1959.

Next in No 54 Sqn's list of Camel aces was G H Hackwill MC with nine victories, including two on FE 2s with No 22 Sqn, as well as the Gotha he shared with C C Banks of No 44 Sqn. He also destroyed a two-seater on the ground. Francis Mansel Kitto, a Welshman born on New Year's Day 1897, had three victories on 'Strutters with No 43 Sqn. Flying Camels with No 54 Sqn, he brought his score to nine, winning the MC. He later flew DH 9 bombers in 1919.

Reginald Stuart Maxwell also ended the war with nine victories. Known as George, he was born on 20 July 1894 and gained his first successes in FE 2s with both Nos 25 and 22 Sqns. Awarded the MC, he was then given command of No 54 Sqn in late 1917, and during 1918 accounted for five German aircraft which brought him the DFC. Post-war Maxwell served in the Middle East, Iraq and Mesopotamia with No 55 Sqn, winning a Bar to his DFC in 1921. On one occasion he was forced to land with engine trouble. Being unable to repair his machine, he had to be rescued by another aircraft, Maxwell lying across its lower wing while it took off. He later served as a squadron commander in Egypt, and in the late 1930s was Station Commander at RAF Mildenhall in England, as a group captain.

No 54 Sqn's standard Camel marking was a single vertical white bar in front of the fuselage roundel, while individual markings took the form of a white number forward of the roundel.

No 65 Sqn

Formed in August 1916, No 65 Sqn eventually went to France with Camels in October 1917. In just a year of air fighting, it claimed around 200 victories of all types, and produced 11 aces.

Chief among them was John Gilmour from Helensburgh, Dumbartonshire, born on 28 June 1896. A former officer with the Argyll and Sutherland Highlanders, he joined the RFC in December 1915. Upon becoming a pilot, Gilmour flew Martinsyde G. 100s on bombing ops with No 27 Sqn from September 1916, although he also accounted for three German aircraft during that September, winning him the MC. Late in 1917 he went to No 65 Sqn as a flight commander, and by December he had become an ace. By early July Gilmour had scored 39 victories, with no fewer than five having been claimed on 1 July 1918. Although often quoted as scoring 44 victories, only 39 of Gilmour's kills can be identified for certain. Thirteen of his victories were made in Camel C8278 and his last 14 in D8118.

Gilmour received two Bars to his MC and then the DSO. Promoted to major, he took command of No 28 Sqn in Italy, but did not add to his score.

He briefly served as air attaché in Rome in July 1919, then went to the Middle East to join No 216 Sqn. Gilmour was offered a

Another high scorer in the final year of the war was Capt John Gilmour DSO MC and two Bars, who scored 36 victories whilst serving as a flight commander with No 65 Sqn. These kills were added to three that he had previously claimed in Martinsyde G.100s whilst with No 27 Sqn in 1916-17

Canadian John White DFC and Bar scored an impressive 22 Camel victories with No 65 Sqn. His final 13 kills were all against the fearsome Fokker D VII, four of which he claimed destroyed in the last big aerial engagement of World War 1, on 4 November 1918. White was killed in a post-war flying accident, on 24 February 1925, whilst serving with the RCAF

Another high scoring ace to serve with No 65 Sqn was Maurice Newnham DFC CdG, who claimed 18 victories between May and November 1918

permanent commission but resigned from the service that December. By 1926 he was working in London.

Canadian Joseph Leonard Maries White – known as John – came from Halifax, where he was born on 6 January 1897. After serving as a machine-gunner, he became a pilot and joined No 65 Sqn in April 1918. From then until war's end he claimed 22 victories, the last 13 of which were all Fokker D VIIs. On 8 August he and his flight had forced down two Fokkers behind Allied lines near Proyart. Receiving the DFC and Bar and CdG, White was involved in the last big combat of the air war on 4 November 1918 when RAF pilots claimed 17 German aircraft shot down – four by White himself. In 1924 he joined the RCAF, only to be killed in a flying accident on 24 February 1925.

Maurice Ashdown Newnham was born in 1897, and he had been a despatch rider with No 4 Sqn in France long before he became a pilot. Once serving with No 65 Sqn, he won the DFC and CdG for scoring an impressive 18 victories between May and November 1918. A group captain in World War 2, Newnham commanded the RAF Parachute Training School and helped train thousands of paratroopers, as well as agents. He died in 1974.

Other aces to serve with No 65 Sqn were T M Williams MC DFC with nine kills, W H Bland and A A Leitch MC DFC with seven, E G Brookes, H L Symons and J A Cunningham with six and G Bremridge AFC, G M Cox MC, E C Eaton and G O Todd with five apiece.

Thomas Mellings Williams came from South Africa, where he was born on 27 September 1899, and he later rose in rank to become Air Marshal Sir Thomas Williams KCB OBE MC DFC MA. Between 1914-16 he served with the 12th South African Infantry in German East Africa. Once trained as a pilot and flying with No 65 Sqn, his nine claims were made over six scouts and three two-seaters. In World War 2 Williams served with Bomber Command (OBE 1941), and then held positions in India and the Far East. Post-war he became Inspector General of the RAF between 1948-51. Knighted (KCB) in 1950, he died on 10 June 1956.

Born on 6 June 1898 in Newbury, Berkshire, William Henry Bland attended Marlborough School and then joined the RFC. By 1918 he was with No 65 Sqn, and whilst flying Camels with the unit he claimed seven Fokker D VII victories and was awarded the CdG.

Alfred Alexander Leitch from Manitoba was known as 'Ack-Ack' due to his initials. Despite suffering from a deformed foot, he became an excellent pilot, serving briefly with No 43 Sqn before going to No 65. Leitch's seven victories with the latter unit won him the MC and DFC. Post-war he flew with the RCAF until 1938, and subsequently passed away on the last day of 1954.

Eric G Brookes, from Bromsgrove, Birmingham, helped John White down those two Fokker D VIIs behind Allied lines on 8 August 1918, thereby bringing his score to six. Later that same day, he failed to return from a patrol and was reported killed. His DFC was announced shortly afterwards.

No 65 Sqn suffered severe casualties on the 8th, with Brookes being killed, another pilot taken prisoner, two others wounded and four more shot-up, three of whom made forced landings. Most of these casualties were caused by ground fire during the course of numerous attack sorties flown in support of the Battle of Amiens, which had commenced that same day.

Edward Eaton, from Montreal, became an ace on 28 May 1918 but on 26 June he in turn fell to the guns of ace Fritz Rumey of *Jasta* 5 – the German's 25th victory. On 23 November the previous year he and others had shared the squadron's first aerial victory.

American George Todd was another participant in the downed D VIIs episode of 8 August, making him an ace. The very next day he was brought down and wounded, crashing in British lines.

Jack Armand Cunningham ended the war as a lieutenant-colonel, having enjoyed a long and successful war. Born in Liverpool on 4 December 1890, he had learnt to fly in 1912 while a lieutenant in the Royal Field Artillery. By 1915 he was flying Vickers 'Gunbuses' and Bristol Scouts with No 18 Sqn, being credited with three kills. After a period with No 6 Sqn and time as an instructor, Cunningham became CO of No 65 Sqn and downed six Albatros Scouts in Camels.

Awarded the DFC and Belgian CdG, he took command of 65 Wing, and on 13 August 1918 used a Camel to shoot down his tenth German aircraft over the Belgian coast. Cunningham received the DSO in the 1919 new year's honours list, and in 1919 he was made a Chevalier of the Order of Leopold by the Belgians and a Chevalier of the *Légion d'Honneur* by the French, who also awarded him the CdG with Palme. Finally, the Belgians presented him with a second Palme for his CdG.

Another ace to fly with No 65 Sqn in the final weeks of the war was A G Jones-Williams MC and Bar. Scoring eight victories in 1917 with No 29 Sqn in Nieuport Scouts, he added three more with No 65 Sqn. Jones-Williams was killed in a flying accident whilst serving as a squadron leader in the RAF in December 1929. In April that same year he had flown non-stop from Cranwell to India in 50 hours.

No 70 Sqn

Formed in April 1916, No 70 Sqn had been the first to equip with Sopwith 1¹/₂ Strutters transferred in from the RNAS. Sent to France, it flew many reconnaissance missions – especially long range sorties far behind the German lines – and saw its share of aerial combat. The unit was briefly mentioned in chapter one, along with two of its early aces, Clive Collett and Noel Webb, but it also had other Camel aces.

No 70 Sqn's top scoring pilot was Francis Grainger Quigley from Toronto, who was born on 10 July 1894. After service in the Canadian Engineers in France, he transferred to the RFC in early 1917, and by that autumn was in France with No 70 Sqn. In the six months from October to March 1918 he claimed 33 victories, which won for him the DSO and MC and Bar. His last 15 kills had been scored in B7475.

An ankle wound ended Quigley's operational flying and he returned to Canada as an instructor. In September he requested a move back to France, but whilst aboard ship he went down with the influenza bug

Scotsman John Todd MC DFC, claimed 18 victories with No 70 Sqn in the first half of 1918

Frank C Gorringe MC, seen here whilst serving as an observer with No 43 Sqn in early 1917, retrained as a pilot and went on to score 14 victories with No 70 Sqn in 1917-18

Oscar Heron DFC, from Northern Ireland, downed 13 aircraft with No 70 Sqn between June and October 1918

that killed tens of thousands in 1918-19, and he died soon after he arrived in Liverpool on 18 October 1918.

John Todd (born on 29 September 1898), from Falkirk, claimed 18 victories in the first half of 1918, 12 of them in Camel C1670. A former medical student at Edinburgh University, he received the MC and DFC before becoming an instructor with No 204 TDS in England. He had joined No 70 Sqn in January 1918, made captain by May and left in July.

Frank Hobson was born on 8 October 1894 in West Bridgford, Nottingham. Serving in the Royal Engineers, he moved to the RFC, and in September 1917 found himself with No 65 Sqn, where he served until early April 1918. Hobson received the MC and then became an instructor with No 72 Training Squadron in England. He left the service in February 1919.

Frank Clifford Gorringe served in three units but scored all 14 of his victories with No 70 Sqn. Born in Eastbourne, Sussex, on 30 September 1889, he was living in Canada when the war began. Gorringe's first taste of combat came as an observer in the rear cockpit of a No 43 Sqn Sopwith 1½ Strutter in 1917. Training as a pilot, he joined No 70 Sqn that autumn, and by the end of the year had become an ace. During the first month and a half of 1918, Gorringe brought his tally to 14, and received the MC.

Following a rest period in England, he returned to France as a flight commander with No 210 Sqn on 25 October. By this stage, many Camel pilots were flying ground attack sorties on a daily basis, and Gorringe was no exception. On one sortie he actually landed right behind advancing British soldiers to tell them exactly where the enemy were. His DFC was gazetted in February 1919. Seven of his victories came in B6426, and most of his claims were of the destroyed variety.

From Armagh, Ireland, came Oscar Aloysius Patrick Heron, born in 1898. After service with the Connaught Rangers, he became a pilot in the RFC and was posted to No 70 Sqn. His 13 victories between June and October 1918 earned him the DFC and Belgian CdG as a flight commander. Ten of his claims were over Fokker D VIIs, eight of them in October alone.

Born on 15 August 1897, Sydney Tyndall Liversedge came from Huddersfield. He had been a trooper in the 1st Life Guards before becoming a pilot. His flying career once he went to France did not get off to a good start, for he was hospitalised twice in just a matter of weeks. However, things improved once Liversedge transferred to No 70 Sqn in early March 1918, and by war's end he had become a flight commander and accounted for 13 aircraft, although he saw out the Armistice from hospital. Liversedge left the service in January 1919.

An engineering student from Glasgow, Walter Macfarlane Carlaw, born on 8 March 1899, joined the RFC in May 1917, and in January 1918 went to No 70 Sqn. He remained with this unit until mid-October, by which time he had scored 12 victories, received the DFC and become a captain. Carlaw's last service days were spent as an instructor in England before leaving the RAF in January 1919. All but two of his claims were over Fokker biplanes, the others being an Albatros Scout and a balloon.

George Robert Howsom from Toronto was born on 21 January 1895. Flying Camels with No 70 Sqn, he shot down 12 German aircraft between December 1917 and March 1918 to win the MC, but a wound on 24 March cut short his war flying. Howsom resumed to the action in late 1918, going to No 43 Sqn, which by then was flying Snipes. His 13th and final victory came on 30 October. He later served in the RCAF and in World War 2 as AOC 4 Training Command. Retiring as an Air Vice-Marshal CBE in 1945, Howsom died on 16 April 1988.

One of the first No 70 Sqn pilots to score a Camel victory was Clive Franklyn Collett from New Zealand, whose biographical details appear in chapter one. Having served as a test pilot, he joined No 70 Sqn in the summer of 1917, and his first Camel victory was over an Albatros D V on 27 July. By early September Collett had achieved 11 victories, his last three claims coming on 9 September. During this engagement he was wounded, possibly by German ace Ludwig Hanstein of *Jasta* 35b. Recovering from his injuries, Collett returned to test flying, but on 23 December, whilst at the controls of a captured Albatros Scout, his aircraft suffered structural failure in flight near Edinburgh and crashed into the Firth of Forth, killing the New Zealander.

Although Alfred Koch was listed as a Canadian, he was actually born in Switzerland on 25 January 1894. His family emigrated to Canada when he was four years old, and when war came he joined the CEF and then the RFC, flying as an observer with Nos 1 and 6 Sqns. Wounded on 22 October 1916, Koch then trained as a pilot, and in the early autumn of 1917 arrived at No 70 Sqn. His ten victories saw him awarded a MC for air fighting and ground attack missions, but a slight wound on 7 March 1918 ended his war flying. He died in the 1980s, having attended a reunion of aviators in 1984 aged 90!

Other Camel aces with No 70 Sqn were K B Watson DFC with nine, Capt Noel Webb MC, who claimed nine of his overall total of 14 with the unit, K G Seth-Smith with seven and E B Booth, D H S Gilbertson, E C Gribben MC, F H Laurence MC, J T Morgan and E H Peverell each with five.

Ken Watson from Ontario scored his ninth and the squadron's last victory on 4 November 1918. Born in 1897, he passed away in 1960. Kenneth Seth-Smith claimed his first victory as an observer whilst No 70 Sqn still had Strutters, but his next six were all on Camels. Formerly with the Northumberland Fusiliers, his run ended when he was wounded on 23 March 1918. Seth-Smith was employed as a test pilot for Hawkers up until he was killed testing a prototype Typhoon on 11 August 1942.

Edward Booth was another ace from Ontario, and his five victories came in late 1917. Injured in a crash on 11 November, he saw no further combat and was subsequently killed in A0131 yet another accident at No 3 TDS in England on 7 April 1918. Dennis Gilbertson, aged 21, was killed in action on 4 September 1918, others in his flight reporting that he had shot down his fifth victory just prior to meeting his death. This particular engagement saw the squadron lose no fewer than eight aircraft to units of JG III near Douai. Born in Hertford but raised in Folkestone pre-war, Gilbertson had attended

Canadian ace George Howsom MC was credited with 12 Camel victories between December 1917 and March 1918 whilst serving with No 70 Sqn. Wounded on 24 March 1918, he eventually returned to the frontline in a Snipe with No 43 Sqn in the final weeks of the war. Howsom claimed his 13th and last victory on 30 October

Swiss Canadian Alfred Koch MC (right) scored ten victories with No 70 Sqn in 1917-18. On the left is Texan H K Boyson, who claimed five Camel kills in Italy with No 66 Sqn. By coincidence, Boyson's middle name was also Koch! (E F Cheesman)

Ranking No 73 Sqn ace was Owen M Baldwin DFC and Bar, who claimed 16 victories between April and September 1918 (*Bruce/Leslie collection*)

Second to Owen in No 73 Sqn in terms of victories was South African G L Graham DFC (left), who was credited with 13 victories. He is seen here posing with French-Canadian Emile J Lussier DFC. A resident of both Canada and the USA, Lussier scored 11 kills with No 73 Sqn between March and November 1918

Wellington College. He fell in flames near the village of Villers-au-Tertre, the local people burying him in their church cemetery.

Edward Gribben came from County Down and had served in the Royal Irish Rifles as a captain prior to learning to fly. In the summer of 1917 he gained five victories with No 70 Sqn and received the MC. Back in England, Gribben spent time with Home Defence and later became a test pilot. Returning to France with No 41 Sqn, he was wounded in action on 2 October 1918 flying an SE 5a, which put him out of the war.

Fred Laurence was serving on No 70 Sqn when the Camels first arrived, and by October 1917 he had become an ace and received the MC. After the war he remained in the RAF and reached the rank of group captain in 1939, retiring from the service at the end of 1945. Fellow ace John Morgan made all of his claims in 1918, the former Royal Welch Fusilier officer from Willesden, London, eventually being killed in a flying accident on 29 October 1918, aged just 20.

Edmund Heaton Peverell from Ilkley, Yorkshire, joined the RFC in April 1917 and gained his five victories in the first few months of 1918. His tour ended in May and he retired from the service in July 1919.

No 73 Sqn

Formed in July 1917 and equipped with Sopwith Camels, No 73 Sqn moved to France in January 1918. As well as performing normal patrol duties, the unit also became involved in heavy ground attack sorties, and for periods it was attached to the Tank Corps in order to fly direct support missions. Air combat resulted in 120 victories being achieved, and ten No 73 Sqn pilots became aces.

The unit's top scorer was Owen Morgan Baldwin, who was born on 21 February 1893 in Twyford. A former mechanical engineer, he became a pilot and joined No 73 Sqn in early 1918 and gained his first victory on 7 April when he downed a Fokker Dr I. Baldwin's scoring rate was modest during the first half of the year, but he became an ace in July and on 15 September he claimed five victories in two patrols. His 16th, and final, claim came on 27 September, by which time he was a flight commander. Of these victories, only three were of the 'out of control' variety. These achievements brought Baldwin the DFC and Bar, as well as France making him a Chevalier of the *Légion d'Honneur*, and awarding him the CdG. He died prematurely on 12 January 1942, aged just 48.

Graham Lynedoch Graham came from Grahamstown, South Africa, where he was born on 18 October 1894. Following service with the 18th Hussars from April 1915 through to August 1916, he transferred to the RFC and became an observer on Strutters with No 70 Sqn, where he served from October 1916 to March 1917. Becoming a pilot, Graham joined No 73 Sqn just as it moved to France, and after the strafing and low bombing attacks during the German March offensive, he downed his first hostile aircraft on 3 May. By 25 August he had scored 13 victories, for which he received the DFC. Like Baldwin,

Graham too was made a Chevalier of the *Légion d'Honneur* and given the CdG. He left the squadron in September and the service in February 1919.

One of the most famous men in the intelligence world first rose to fame as a Camel ace with No 73 Sqn. Canadian William Samuel Stephenson from Winnipeg (born on 11 January 1896) had served with the Canadian Engineers until he was badly gassed in France

while a sergeant, although he remained with his unit throughout 1916. Transferring to the RFC, he was commissioned and joined No 73 Sqn. Stephenson's first period in action during the March 1918 battles won him the MC, to which he added the DFC later in the year. He downed his 12th victory on 28 July, but in a later fight with some Fokkers was brought down himself and taken prisoner, the third victory (of ten) of Ltn Justus Grassmann of *Jasta* 10. Although wounded he survived the crash.

After the war Stephenson became a successful businessman, but both before and during World War 2 he played a prominent part in counter-intelligence work in North America. He was Churchill's Personal Representative and Director of Security Coordination in the Western Hemisphere between 1940-46. For his services Stephenson was knighted by King George VI, while the Americans gave him the US Presidential Medal for Merit. He died on 31 January 1989 in Bermuda.

Canadian William S Stephenson MC DFC was credited with 12 victories between March and July 1918, when he was shot down by German ace Ltn Justus Grassmann of *Jasta* 10 and made a PoW. He is seen here standing alongside his battle-weathered No 73 Sqn Camel D6476

No 73 Sqn ace Emile Lussier poses with Camel D9438 in which he scored his first three victories in July 1918

William Henry Hubbard was another Canadian, born in Kingston, Ontario, on 19 May 1896. He joined the RFC in 1916 and served with Nos 7 and 5 Sqns flying BE 2s. On 8 September he and his observer engaged a Fokker monoplane, which they claimed as being destroyed. Wounded on 26 December, Hubbard returned to England and then became an instructor. In 1918 he went back to France upon being posted to No 73 Sqn, and by the end of hostilities had added ten more kills to his tally, and received the DFC and Bar. Hubbard also flew many ground attack missions. He passed away on 19 June 1960.

Emile John Lussier, who was, as his name suggests, a French-Canadian, was born in Chicago, on 10 October 1895. He resided in Illinois for 15 years before moving to Canada in 1910 with his family, and was living in Alberta when war came. Giving his address as Medicine Hat, he joined the RFC in Canada and flew Camels from March 1918, shooting down 11 German aircraft by the Armistice. Lussier was awarded the DFC primarily for an action on 25 August in which he accounted for three Fokker D VIIs in two engagements. He became a flight commander in October 1918.

After the war Lussier returned to America, where he became a farmer, but in World War 2 he again joined the RCAF and served as a squadron leader in various wireless schools. Moving back to the USA post-war, he returned to farming until he retired in Westminster, Maryland. He died 11 December 1974. Despite his parentage, the Americans consider Lussier to be one of their aces.

Other aces to serve with No 73 Sqn were R N Chandler DFC, N Cooper DFC, M LeBlanc-Smith DFC, T S Sharpe DFC and G E H Pidcock. Robert 'Chubby' Chandler from Leyton joined the RFC in March 1917 and got to No 73 Sqn nine months later. He won the DFC for his seven victories and ground attack sorties, and left the service in May 1919. Emigrating to Canada, Chandler later served in the RCAF in World War 2, retiring as a wing commander.

American Norman Cooper, whose real name was E S Tooker, served as a private in the Canadian Army from June 1916 to August 1917, then trained as an RFC pilot. His six victories won him the DFC, his citation also relating how, on 3 October 1918, he observed a German position holding up an advance by Allied soldiers. In a series of diving attacks Cooper drove the Germans out of their trenches, enabling the advance to continue.

Maurice LeBlanc-Smith was a veteran RFC pilot long before he joined No 73 Sqn as a flight commander. Born in Leatherhead, Surrey, in 1896, he flew Vickers FB 5 two-seater fighters in 1915-16 and later DH 2s. After a period as an instructor, he went to No 73 Sqn and gained six victories and a DFC in 1918. LeBlanc-Smith died on 29 October 1986. When I contacted him in 1974, he wanted to make it clear exactly what the squadron's badge – a dog looking into a cupboard, partly surrounded by the letter 'C' – was all about. It had been previously described as CO Maj T O'B Hubbard's (not related to W H Hubbard) dog, with the 'C' standing for the Canadian personnel on the squadron. He wrote;

'The mistake over the origin of the No 73 Sqn crest is being perpetuated. The crest was designed at the outset by Eric Wardnum,

Surrey-born Maurice LeBlanc-Smith DFC served in the RFC from 1915 until war's end, and claimed all six of his victories with No 73 Sqn

one of our original pilots, with whom I shared a hut at our first airfield in France, Estrees Blanche (also known as Liettres). Maj Hubbard did not take a dog to France – the allusion was simply to the nursery rhyme – and the "C" had nothing to do with Canadians. Indeed, we only had one I think, until much later. It stood, of course, for Camel. It seems to me so obvious that I can't imagine who invented the other version. At first, this squadron badge was on all our Camels until stopped by HQ for giving our identity away to the enemy too easily.'

Thomas Sydney Sharpe from Gloucester had flown with No 24 Sqn in 1916, and in 1918 he went to No 73 Sqn as a flight commander. All six of his victories were scored in March 1918, prior to him being shot down by Manfred von Richthofen on the 27th – the Baron's 71st victory. Once it was known that Sharpe had survived, the award of the DFC was put in hand and later awarded. Returning from prison camp at the end of the war, he ran a building company for many years in his home county.

Geoffrey Pidcock was another experienced pilot, having flown with Nos 60, 44 Home Defence and 1 Sqns, before becoming a flight commander with No 73 Sqn. To his one victory with No 60 Sqn he added six more with No 73 Sqn, receiving the CdG. He remained in the RAF after the war, rising to Air Vice-Marshal CB CBE and being made a Commander of the US Legion of Merit. He died on 12 February 1976.

No 80 Sqn

Formed in August 1917, this unit also moved to France in January 1918 in time to play an active ground attack role opposing the German March offensive. Like No 73 Sqn, No 80 was also tasked to support the Tank Corps, engaging any would-be anti-tank gun opposition these metal monsters encountered during attacks. Heavy casualties were sustained by the squadron in this role, and aerial combat opportunities were few and far between. However, the unit's one ace scored no fewer than 23 victories out of the squadron's overall tally of 60.

He was Harold Alfred Whistler, born on 30 December 1896. Having attended the Royal Military College at Sandhurst, and been commissioned into the Dorsetshire Regiment, he then transferred to the RFC in 1916. Whistler flew with No 3 Sqn in that same year, but was wounded on 29 January 1917. Later that autumn he joined No 80 Sqn as a flight commander and became its most outstanding combat pilot. He received the DSO, DFC and Bar, and received a Mention in

Flight commander Harold A Whistler DSO DFC and two Bars was easily No 80 Sqn's most outstanding fighter pilot, claiming 23 of the unit's 60 kills by war's end. Indeed, he was also No 80 Sqn's solitary ace!

South African Christopher 'Flossie' Quintin-Brand DSO MC was No 151 Sqn's CO, and its sole ace. He led the specialist Camel nightfighter unit from its formation in June 1918 until war's end, adding four kills to his previous tally of seven on Nieuport Scouts with No 1 Sqn in 1917 and one with a Camel (again at night) with No 112 Sqn on Home Defence patrols in May 1918

Also from South Africa, D'Urban V Armstrong DFC claimed four night kills with No 151 Sqn to add to his solitary victory whilst serving with No 60 Sqn (Nieuport Scouts) in 1916. A veteran of more than two years of combat, he was killed barely 48 hours after the Armistice when he crashed his Camel whilst performing impromptu low-level aerobatics

Despatches. Most of Whistler's claims were over fighters, with the exception of one balloon and three two-seaters. On 1 June 1918 the plywood behind his seat was set on fire by a tracer bullet, but he managed to beat out the flames and fly home safely.

Whistler remained in the RAF post-war, and at one stage was an instructor at Cranwell. In 1929 he won a second Bar to his DFC for operations against Najd bedouin tribesmen while commanding No 55 Sqn in Iraq in 1927-28. In the early 1930s he instructed at the Central Flying School and later became a wing commander. Whistler served in Iraq, then with Fighter Command, attended the Imperial Defence College and, from 1937, spent time in India as an instructor at the Staff College at Quetta. He was killed in a flying accident over the Persian Gulf whilst flying back to England in an Imperial Airways *Hannibal* airliner on 1 March 1940, Whistler heading home to accept promotion to air commodore.

The No 80 Sqn marking was a vertical white bar just in front of the tailplane which was repeated on the upper starboard wing, while its various flights employed different wheel covers in red, white and blue respectively. Individual letters were used in front of the cockade until around May/June 1918, when these were moved aft of the national marking.

No 151 Sqn

A dedicated nightfighter unit, No 151 Sqn was formed to operate over France, being created in June 1918. It moved to the continent that same month, being led by Maj C J Quintin-Brand MC, who proved to be its only ace. No 151 Sqn's kills totalled 21 by war's end.

'Flossie' Brand was a South African from Kimberley, born on 25 May 1893, and after army service he joined the RFC in 1916. Flying Nieuports with No 1 Sqn he claimed seven victories during the early months of 1917, then became a Home Defence pilot. Serving with No 112 Sqn, Brand claimed his first night kill on 19 May, and once with No 151 in France, he downed four more to become a Camel ace. All five kills came whilst flying D6423. These brought Brand's war total to 12. He remained in the RAF post-war, and in 1920 he and Pierre van Ryneveld MC flew from England to Cape Town in 109 hours after many adventures. Both were knighted for their achievements. In World War 2 Brand commanded a fighter group during the Battle of Britain and retired in 1943 as an Air Vice-Marshal KBE DSO DFC MC. He died in Rhodesia on 9 March 1968.

A near Camel ace with No 151 Sqn was D'Urban Victor Armstrong, also from South Africa. He had claimed one victory flying with No 60 Sqn in late 1916 (on Nieuports), and became an ace by scoring four night victories in C6713 with No 151 Sqn. He nearly made it five on 23 September 1918 when he attacked a German two-seater over Havrincourt Wood. The observer was seen to fall out, but the action was judged indecisive by wing HQ. Sadly, Armstrong was killed in a low-level aerobatic display two days after the Armistice in this same Camel. He had just been awarded the DFC.

AUSTRALIANS, AMERICANS AND CAMELS OVER ITALY

The Australian Flying Corps (AFC) established four frontline squadrons to fight in World War 1, No 1 Sqn AFC (with various bomber types and then the Bristol F 2b Fighter) in Palestine and the Middle East, No 2 Sqn AFC (which eventually had SE5as) on the Western Front, No 3 Sqn AFC which was a Corps squadron in France with RE 8s, and No 4 Sqn AFC with Camels.

The latter unit had started life as No 71 Sqn RFC in March 1917. After several months of training and 'working up', it was fully equipped with Camels and sent to France in December, becoming No 4 Sqn AFC on 20 January 1918. In all, the unit had scored around 220 victories by war's end, and produced 11 aces.

Its top scorer was Capt Arthur Henry Cobby from Melbourne (born on 26 August 1894). A bank clerk pre-war, he had joined the AFC in December 1916 and been posted to No 71 Sqn/No 4 Sqn AFC, where he opened his tally during the German March offensive in 1918. Cobby was said to be an aggressive yet cunning pilot, who engaged aircraft, attacked balloons and strafed ground targets at every possible opportunity. He received the DFC and two Bars, became a flight

A H Cobby DSO DFC and two Bars claimed 29 victories with the Camel whilst serving with No 4 Sqn AFC

commander and, just as he was rested on 4 September, was presented with the DSO. Cobby was the highest scoring AFC pilot with 29 victories, which included five balloons. Fourteen of his kills were scored in D1929 and at least nine more in E1416 – the latter aircraft was also used by fellow ace E R King to down five aircraft.

Cobby served in the RAAF post-war, and had been made a wing commander by 1933. He left the air force three years later to become Controller of Operations with the Civil Aviation Board. Back in uniform come World War 2, Cobby was initially involved in recruiting and later as an operational commander in Western Australia, where he was awarded the GM for his actions on 7 September 1943. A passenger in a Catalina flying-boat, he was injured in a crash-landing but succeeded in playing a major part in rescuing survivors. Later Cobby commanded the RAAF Staff College, led an operational group in the South-west Pacific from July 1944 and left the service as an Air Commodore CBE to return to civil aviation. He died on Armistice Day 1955.

In his book *High Adventure*, Cobby described one fight which occurred on 15 July 1918. Flying in company with H G Watson, they encountered some Pfalz Scouts over Armentiéres;

'They were flying in company south-east from the line towards that much-battered town at 6000 ft, and my partner and I climbed above the clouds from farther east and flew towards them. The clouds were scattered cumulus, and when we had gone far enough we put down our noses and went through them flat out – Wattie's wing tip was almost up against mine. We came out a little to the east and slightly above the Germans and immediately attacked. There was a crowd of other enemy scouts about at the time, including some "tripes" – a type we had not seen for some time, but they couldn't have noticed us. We were almost behind the Pfalz, and turning slightly while diving, came down onto the tails of the two rear ones, and with my first burst sent my opponent down in flames. Wattie's fire must have been accurate, as his man went up nose first until the machine stalled, then went down in a spin.

'I did not watch it for long, as I went through on to the next machine on my side, opening fire at once and putting in a long burst as I came up on him. He half-rolled at once and I zoomed up over him and turned to fire again, but it was unnecessary, as the right-hand wing had collapsed and the machine fell to pieces. I was startled by the familiar pop-pop-pop-pop of machine-guns from above, and glancing over my shoulder saw the "tripe" formation coming down on us. Wattie also shot past me on a "split-arse" turn, firing his guns to attract my attention to the danger, and pointing upwards. I shook my head and pointed downwards, indicating "nothing doing", then kicked my bus into a half-roll, pulled the stick back into my tummy and went into the clouds in a vertical dive and kept in it for about 4000 ft before easing it out. This manoeuvre was not as dangerous from an attack point of view as it may seen, as the triplane was notoriously weak structurally, and would break up at excessive speeds.'

With only three fewer kills than Cobby, Elwyn Roy King from Bathurst, New South Wales (born on 13 May 1894), was the

Capt H G Watson DFC (left) claimed 14 victories and Capt E J K McCloughry DSO DFC and Bar 21 kills, both aces flying with No 4 Sqn AFC

next highest scorer. 'Bo' King volunteered, like so many of his countrymen, to serve with the Australian Light Horse, leaving his engineering job, but then moved to the AFC. Joining No 4 Sqn AFC in France, his first claim came on 20 May 1918, and by early October his tally had run to 19. With the arrival of the Snipe, King added a further seven kills to his score to become the type's highest scoring pilot of the war. His deeds brought him the DSO and DFC. Once back in Australia, King returned to the engineering business, although he served again in World War 2. Indeed, it was whilst CO of RAAF Point Cook that he died on 28 November 1941 following a short illness.

There could not have been many air aces whose brother commanded the unit in which he fought, but Edgar James Kingston McCloughry was one. Edgar, later known as Kingston-McCloughry, was born on 10 September 1896 in Adelaide. He joined the Australian Engineers prior to transferring to the AFC in December 1916, and his first tour was spent flying SPADs with No 23 Sqn in France. Injured in a crash, McCloughry instructed for a while, before becoming a flight commander with No 4 Sqn AFC in France. His first kill was over a balloon on 12 June 1918, followed minutes later by a Pfalz Scout. By month end he was an ace, and in July his tally increased to 17.

After a short rest following a wound sustained on 31 July, McCloughry added four more scalps in September to bring his total to 21. All but these last four were scored whilst flying D1961, a machine later shot down by ground fire during an airfield attack on 17 August, but not whilst being flown by McCloughry. Being wounded yet again on 24 September (this time whilst strafing a train), shortly after gaining his last two victories, ended his war. Some of his fellow pilots consider a few of his claims doubtful, but the record remains. McCloughry did, however, receive the DSO, DFC and Bar. Post-war, he attended the Staff College while in the RAF, and later commanded No 4 Sqn RAF, and in World War 2 he held various posts. McCloughry retired as an air vice-marshal in 1953, and died on 15 November 1972.

Herbert Gillies Watson was a New Zealander, born in Dunedin on 30 March 1889, but was working as a depot manager in Sydney when war came, so he enlisted in the Australian ASC. He moved to the AFC in 1917 and trained in England, going to No 4 Sqn AFC in France in February 1918. His 14 kills, including three balloons, came between

19 April and 2 October, winning for him the DFC and a flight commander's post. Watson left as the Snipes arrived, his tour over. Post-war he bred racehorses in Victoria, and died in the early 1940s.

Another Australian to score with both the Camel and the Snipe was Thomas Charles Richmond Baker, born on 2 May 1897 in Smithfield, South Australia. When war came he was a bank clerk, but he enlisted into the artillery in July 1915, and in December 1916 was awarded the Military Medal (MM) for bravery in France, mending telephone lines under fire. For further heroism he received a Bar to this decoration.

Moving to the AFC in September 1917, Baker was posted to No 4 Sqn AFC in June 1918, and he shot down six German aircraft with Camels and a further six with Snipes. On 4 November he was one of two No 4 Sqn AFC aces shot down in a battle with *Jasta* 2, both of whom fell to unit CO Karl Bolle – these were the German ace's 35th and 36th, and last, victories.

Leonard Thomas Eaton Taplin claimed all 12 of his victories on Camels with No 4 Sqn AFC. Born in Adelaide on 16 December 1895, he had worked as an electrical engineer prior to joining the Australian Army. Transferring to the AFC, he served with No 1 Sqn AFC in Palestine, then on coming to England, was sent to No 4 Sqn AFC in July 1918. Taplin had gained one kill (on 17 July) when he narrowly escaped death on the 26th. Taking off with bombs on a strafing sortie, his Camel's axle snapped. Rapidly switching off his engine, he undid his safety belt, and as his Camel (C8226) touched down again, the bombs exploded and he was catapulted clear without injury!

Ten of Taplin's next eleven victories came in E1407, which he was duly shot down in on 5 September and taken prisoner. He and his patrol had been engaged by *staffeln* from JG III, which shot down four of the five Camels. Taplin had recently been awarded the DFC, and four of his victories had been balloons.

Camel B2489 of No 4 Sqn AFC was a presentation machine, christened *New South Wales No 6*. Lt A E Robertson claimed four victories with it in March 1918. Although some sources credit this pilot with seven victories, four seems to be the correct number (*Bruce/Leslie collection*)

Other Camel aces in the squadron were T H Barkell DFC, G Jones DFC, A J Palliser and N C Trescowthick, all with seven kills, and G F Malley with six. Thomas Barkell, from Sydney, claimed his victories in the last months of the war before being wounded in the leg on 29 October. He was awarded the DFC, and post-war went into commercial flying. George Jones, from Victoria, also won the DFC for his skill, claiming three kills on Camels and three on Snipes. I mention him because he became an Air Marshal KBE CB, and when he died on 24 August 1992, he was the last surviving Australian ace of World War 1, aged 95.

Arthur John Palliser is also mentioned, despite only claiming two Camel victories, for he added five Snipe victories to his tally before he fell in combat on 4 November, along with T C R Baker. Garnet 'Garnie' Malley got all his victories on Camels, and won an early MC with the squadron for actions during the March battles of 1918. Born in Sydney in 1892, he had previously been a mechanic.

17th Aero Squadron USAS

American aviation volunteers came in several guises in World War 1, some going to the French via the Lafayette Flying Corps, some directly into the RFC, either via Canada or coming to England, while others joined the US Aviation Service (USAS) of the Signal Corps. Most of the latter eventually came to England to complete their American flight training, and some wound up with RAF units in order to gain combat experience while their own air service began to arrive in France. Others, however, were posted to two newly-formed USAS Camel squadrons, and of these a number remained in this unit for several months.

The 17th was formed in the USA in 1917, and came under RAF control in July 1918 as part of the 65 Wing. Its pilots claimed over 60 victories, and five aces were produced. H Burdick claimed eight, H C Knotts seven, G A Vaughn six (of an eventual 13), L A Hamilton five (of a total of ten), as did R M Todd. The unit had 13 pilots killed and six taken prisoner, the largest single loss being inflicted during a fight with JG III on 26 August when six Camels were shot down.

Howard Burdick was born on 12 December 1891 in Brooklyn, New York. His eight victories won him the British DFC. In World War 2 his son Clinton (born in Brooklyn in 1924) was a fighter ace too, flying P-51D Mustangs with the USAAF's 361st Fighter Squadron/356th Fighter Group in 1944-45 as part of the Eighth Air Force in England. His score was listed as 5.5 kills, and he won the American DFC. Burdick senior died in Los Angeles, California, in January 1975.

Howard Knotts destroyed more German aircraft as a PoW than as a fighter pilot! Born in Illinois on 25 August 1895, he trained in Canada and the USA, before joining the 17th Aero in August 1918. His six combat victories were all Fokker D VIIs, which brought him the DFC and the American DSC. However, Knotts was shot down and captured on 14 October, and while on a train journey to his prison camp, he

Howard C Knotts was credited with shooting down six Fokker D VIIs whilst serving with the 17th US Aero Squadron in 1918. He was shot down and captured on 14 October

managed to set fire to a train he saw laden with Fokker biplanes, causing enough damage to write off seven of them. For this act he was almost executed by firing squad but got away with it. Post-war, Knotts became a noted aviation lawyer, but died from a heart attack on 23 November 1942.

George A Vaughn Jr from Brooklyn, New York (born on 20 May 1897), scored six Camel victories as a flight commander following a successful spell on SE 5as with No 84 Sqn RAF. He won the British DFC and the US DSC. An aeronautical engineer post-war, he died on 31 July 1989 from a brain tumour. Born in Troy, New York, on 13 June 1894, Lloyd A Hamilton was another who became an ace with the RAF – he scored five kills flying Camels with No 3 Sqn – before joining the 17th. A further five kills took his Camel claims to ten, and he too won the DFC and American DSC. He was killed in action on 24 August 1918 when brought down by ground fire.

Robert M Todd was an ace with five victories, although his last two were claimed for him on 26 August 1918 – a day which saw him shot

Elliott White Springs was the ranking ace of the 148th Aero Squadron, claiming 12 of his 16 kills with Camels whilst serving with the USAS unit. His remaining four kills came on SE 5as during his brief attachment to No 85 Sqn in early 1918

Field E Kindley also claimed 12 Camel victories, 11 with the 148th Aero Squadron and one with No 65 Sqn

The 148th's Henry C Clay Jr was credited with eight victories. He died during the influenza epidemic in February 1919

down in a fight with *Jasta* 27 in one of six aircraft lost by the squadron that day, Todd becoming a PoW. Post-war he went into engineering, but in World War 2 he served in the USAAF in both the USA and in England. He died on 20 January 1988.

The 17th Aero's unit markings consisted of a white dumbbell on the fuselage sides aft of the roundel, with individual letters ahead of it.

148th Aero Squadron USAS

Formed in Texas in late 1917, the 148th Aero also became part of the RAF's 65 Wing in the summer of 1918. Its pilots scored 47 victories, with 19 other aircraft being driven down out of control. The unit produced five aces, with Elliott White Springs being its top scorer.

Springs, famous for his post-war writings on aviation, was born in South Carolina on 31 July 1896. Yet another 'Yank' to fly SE 5as with the RAF in the early summer of 1918, he claimed four kills with No 85 Sqn. Later, as a flight commander with the 148th, he boosted his score to 16, and won the DFC and American DSC. Barnstorming after the war, and then joining his father's cotton mills, Springs also served in World War 2. He died from cancer on 15 October 1959.

Field E Kindley from Pea Ridge, Arkansas (born on 13 March 1896), had started his working life as a motion picture operator. Joining the war effort in 1917, he found himself attached to No 65 Sqn in May 1918. Kindley then went to the 148th as a flight commander. He had scored one victory with the RAF, and he followed this up with 11 kills with his new unit, gaining the

Jessie O Creech received the British DFC for his seven victories with the 148th Aero Squadron

Six-victory ace Clayton L Bissell of the 148th Aero Squadron remained in the Army Air Corps post-war and rose to the rank of major-general in World War 2

Lt C M McEwen MC DFC (right) claimed 27 victories with No 28 Sqn in Italy, while Capt N C Jones DFC (left) was credited with nine kills with Nos 28 and 45 Sqns (*Bruce/Leslie collection*)

Capt W G Barker ended the war with 50 victories and the VC, DSO and Bar and MC and two Bars. Of these kills, the Canadian ace claimed 46 of them whilst flying Camel B6313 with Nos 28, 66 and 139 Sqns

DSC and Oak Leaf Cluster (bar), as well as the British DFC. Post-war, he took command of the 94th Pursuit Squadron in Texas, but was killed in a flying accident on 1 February 1920.

Henry R Clay Jr with eight, Jesse O Creech with seven victories and Clayton L Bissell with six were the unit's other aces. Clay also flew with the RAF's No 43 Sqn before going to the 148th. From Missouri, he received the DFC and DSC but died during the great influenza epidemic on 17 February 1919. Jesse Creech came from Washington DC, although he had been born in Kentucky. The British gave him the DFC for his seven claims, plus one unconfirmed. He died in February 1948. Clay Bissell, from Pennsylvania, also received the DFC and remained in the USAAC post-war, becoming a major-general and serving in the CBI during World War 2. He became air attaché in London, prior to his death in September 1972.

CAMELS OVER ITALY

The three Camel squadrons sent to Italy to support the Italians in their fight against the Austro-Hungarians had all seen service in France in 1917. Despite its low number, No 28 Sqn, formed in late 1915, had remained in England until it moved to France in October 1917 with Camels. It saw action during the Third Battle of Ypres, but was then sent to Italy, where it served throughout 1918. No 28 Sqn claimed 136 victories and boasted 11 aces by war's end, C M McEwen being its top scorer.

Clifford Mackay 'Black Mike' McEwen was born in Manitoba on 2 July 1897. He joined the RFC via the Canadian Army in June 1917, and scored his first victory with No 28 Sqn on 30 December. On 4 October 1918 he downed victory number 27, having by then received the MC, DFC and Italian Bronze Medal for Military Valour. McEwen's victory on 18 February 1918, claimed by him as 'out of control', was confirmed many years later when the wreckage was finally discovered in the Italian mountains. He joined the RCAF after the war and became an air vice-marshal, commanding No 6 Bomber Group late on in World War 2. McEwen died on 6 August 1967.

Also from Manitoba (born on 3 November 1894), the amazing William George 'Billy' Barker served in the Canadian Mounted Rifles from 1914 and saw action in the trenches. He then became an RFC observer, and later learnt to fly. Posted back to a two-seater unit as a pilot, Barker won a Bar to the MC he had received when an observer. Then, as a Camel pilot and flight commander with No 28 Sqn in France, he scored three victories, followed by a further 19 in Italy. He then moved to No 66 Sqn, again as flight commander, and added 16 more kills to his tally, gaining a second Bar to his MC, plus a DSO and the Italian Silver Medal. Given command of No 139 Sqn, which flew Bristol F 2b Fighters, he took his Camel with him and used it to increase his score to 46, for which he was awarded a Bar to his DSO.

He flew the same Camel – B6313 – throughout this period, the aircraft becoming almost as famous as Barker himself. The aircraft had flown with Nos 28, 66 and 139 Sqns in both France and Italy, and its Canadian pilot had used it to claim no fewer than 46 victories. It was easily the highest scoring Camel of World War 1.

The most successful Camel of them all – 'Billy' Barker's famous B6313

In this earlier view of B6313, the fighter reveals the No 28 Sqn white square marking on its top wing, along with the Camel's individual number '1'. The three pilots standing in front of the aircraft are aces 'Billy' Barker, Harold Hudson and James Mitchell (*Bruce/Leslie collection*)

Returning to England as an instructor, Barker managed to persuade 'the powers' to allow him to spend time in France to bring himself up to date with the 'latest developments', and in a famous action on 27 October 1918, he was credited with four victories while flying a Snipe. However, he was severely wounded in this action, but it brought him the award of the Victoria Cross. After the war he went into civil aviation and then served in the RCAF until 1924. Made vice president of the Fairchild Aviation Corporation of Canada, Barker died in a flying accident on 12 March 1930.

A pilot who often flew with Barker in No 28 Sqn was fellow Canadian Harold Byron Hudson from Victoria, British Columbia, although he was born in Surrey, England, on 8 December 1898 – he had emigrated to Canada in 1912 with his family. Returning to serve with the RFC in Italy, he accounted for seven balloons and six aircraft, several of which he shared with Barker. Hudson won the MC and after a brief period with No 45 Sqn, returned to England. He died in February 1982.

James Hart 'Mitch' Mitchell was a Yorkshireman who had served in the Essex Regiment prior to joining the RFC in 1917. He was sent to No 28 Sqn as the unit moved to France, and like Barker, had three victories by the time he was sent to Italy. Mitchell was made a flight commander, and before returning to Home Establishment in July 1918, he had scored 11 victories. He won the MC, DFC and the Italian Bronze Medal.

Capt James Mitchell MC DFC (11 victories) of No 28 Sqn used B6344 to score six of his kills. This aircraft features identical markings to those previously worn on 'Billy' Barker's B6313 before it became 'G' (*Bruce/Leslie collection*)

Yet another Canadian, this time from Montreal, Stanley Stanger was born on 10 July 1894. His early military career included a spell with the US National Guard, the 50th Westmount Rifles and the 4th Canadian Ammunition Supply Park attached to the 1st Canadian Artillery. In May 1917 Stanger was commissioned into the RFC, and he joined No 66 Sqn in October, serving both in France and in Italy, where he gained three victories before moving to No 28 Sqn on 27 April 1918 as a flight commander. He claimed a further ten victories and received the MC and DFC. Wounded by flak on 23 August, Stanger was back in action a month later. One day in October he became unwell in the air and landed by mistake on an Austrian airfield. He had switched off his engine before he realised his predicament, but by using his flying boots as wheel chocks, managed to swing the propeller, climb back into the cockpit and take off before being captured. Once back in Canada, Stanger joined the family business in Montreal, becoming its president in 1939. He died on 10 September 1967.

John Mackereth claimed six kills with Nos 28 and 66 Sqns. He is seen here posing in front of B6344 'G' of No 28 Sqn (*Bruce/Leslie collection*)

Camel B6363 of No 28 Sqn was credited with eight victories, five of these being scored by Capt P Wilson in the first half of 1918 and three by R G Hallonquist in June and July of that same year (*Phil Jarrett*)

Other No 28 Sqn aces were A G Cooper, P Wilson MC and J Mackereth with seven apiece, T F Williams with six (14 altogether) and J E Hallonquist DFC and A G Jarvis with five each. John Mackereth was unlucky enough to down an Austrian pilot who had been dropping messages over the Allied lines reporting on lost RAF airmen. With five victories, he became a flight commander in No 66 Sqn, but was brought down, wounded, on 31 August 1918 and taken prisoner after flaming a balloon for his seventh victory.

Arthur Cooper was born in Essex in 1898 and had been a student until he joined the RFC in April 1917. He received the Italian *Croce di Guerra* and ended the war as a Home Defence pilot in England. Cooper was killed in a civil air crash at Weymouth on 29 May 1928.

Thomas Frederic Williams, from Ontario (born on 12 October 1885), was older than most of his contemporaries. After service with the Canadian army, he transferred to the RFC in England and was sent to No 45 Sqn, where he scored eight kills over France and Italy. Moving to No 28 Sqn as a flight commander, he added six to his tally, winning the MC and Italian Bronze Medal. Williams was recommended for the DFC but did not receive it. A barnstormer in the 1920s, he became chief test pilot for the Fleet Aircraft Company in Ontario, and was still flying in his late 80s. He died in July 1985, aged 99. I was in touch with 'Voss' Williams in the late 1960s;

'Perhaps the funniest action I had was in Italy. We had just had a fight north of Venice at about 12,000-13,000 ft, disposing of a Hun, when I thought I saw a movement close to the ground. I glued my eyes on the spot and dived. It was a scout flying towards our balloon lines. My Aldis sight fogged up and I had no ring sight on either gun. At about 5000 ft above him I touched one of the triggers to see, by a tracer round, how good I was at guessing the deflection – I fired about three rounds. He turned 180 degrees and I touched the trigger again to get the opposite deflection – about another three rounds – at not less than 3000 ft from him. Instantly his ship went down like a pack of cards. As I climbed up to rejoin our formation, I wondered where he would fall. I put a ring with my pencil around the area which enclosed the town of Meola.

'Later that day I flew over that area but could find no trace of the crashed aircraft. Meola was in the Italian area on our side of the lines. I got a ribbing for claiming a victory in our lines that couldn't be found. Some time later I was en route to England when I got into conversation with a war correspondent on my train. He told me of writing about an event on this same date when a Hun machine (from *Flik* 12D) fell into a house in Meola, burning it and killing the old lady inside. I told him it must have been the Hun we could not find. Immediately the man got up and never spoke to me again.'

Joe Hallonquist from Mission City, British Columbia, served with the Canadian artillery prior to joining the RAF. He scored five victories, plus a sixth which wing HQ disallowed, and received the DFC and Italian Bronze Medal. He became a PoW on 29 October 1918, brought down due to hitting a truck while ground strafing. Taken to hospital, Hallonquist was left behind during the enemy retreat and made his escape. A post-war insurance salesman, he died in

Canadian Capt T F Williams MC claimed 14 victories with Nos 45 and 28 Sqns over France and Italy. He passed away in July 1985, just a few months short of his 100th birthday

August 1958 in Moose Jaw. Born in Suffolk, but living in London, Arthur Jarvis served with No 28 Sqn in France and Italy. He remained in the RAF until 1929, and served again in World War 2, ending the war a Group Captain OBE AFC.

No 45 Sqn

Formed in March 1916, No 45 Sqn went to France that October with Sopwith 1¹/₂ Strutters and saw considerable action before re-equipping with Camels in July 1917. It had just started operating with the fighter when the move to Italy came. Over the Italian Front, it saw a good deal more action until it returned to France in September 1918 to become a long-range escort to the Independent Air Force (IAF). However, the war ended before it could start this role. No 45 Sqn's overall tally of victories amounted to 316.

The unit's top ace was Matthew Brown 'Bunty' Frew, born in Glasgow on 7 April 1895. He had served with the Highland Light Infantry in France prior to moving to the RFC in August 1916, and by April 1917 he was with No 45 Sqn flying Strutters. Frew and his observers had claimed five victories prior to the arrival of the Camel. Paired up with the new Sopwith scout, his claimed a further 18 victories (11 in France and seven in Italy) to take his overall tally to 23. Frew's rewards were the DSO, MC and Bar, plus the Italian Silver Medal. Suffering a neck injury during a forced landing, he had to return to England in February 1918, and he became an instructor.

In 1931-32 Frew saw action in Kurdistan, adding a Bar to his DSO, and later led RAF squadrons in England. He held various posts in World War 2, reaching the rank of air vice-marshal in 1948 with the KBE, CB, AFC, Greek Royal Order of George I with Swords, and the Belgian CdG. He retired to Pretoria, where he died in May 1974. I was in contact with 'Bunty' Frew in 1967, when he told me;

'I was posted to No 45 Sqn at St Marie Capelle, where I flew Sopwith two-seaters. In July the squadron was re-equipped with

Capt M B Frew DSO MC and Bar (left) scored 23 victories with No 45 Sqn, 18 of them on Camels. He is seen here with B6372, which he used to claim at least 12 of his victories (*Bruce/Leslie collection*)

Camels, which although difficult to fly were wonderful aircraft. In late December 1917 the squadron was moved from France to Italy, where I served until I received a direct hit from an anti-aircraft shell. Although my aircraft was very badly damaged, I managed to land safely a few hundred yards behind our frontlines. On the patrol before I was hit I shot down four enemy aircraft (only two allowed by wing). Unfortunately, the doctors discovered I had displaced my head during my crash-landing, and I was posted home.'

Australian Cedric Ernest 'Spike' Howell was born in Adelaide on 17 June 1896. Having served with the ANZACs in Gallipoli and France, he transferred to the RFC. Posted to No 45 Sqn, Howell claimed all 19 of his kills in Italy, being awarded the DSO, MC and DFC. Rested in July, he saw no further action. On 10 December 1919, whilst taking part in the London to Australia flight in a Martinsyde-Rolls aircraft, Howell and his mechanic died in a crash off St George's Bay, Corfu.

Born in Plymouth, Devon, on 19 June 1892, Jack Cottle spent his early life in Zululand. When war came, he joined the South African Mounted Rifles, serving in this unit in German East Africa until he decided to transfer to the RFC. Posted to No 45 Sqn in Italy, he remained with the unit through to the Armistice, except for a period off duty following a wound on 30 May 1918. Scoring 11 victories in Italy, Cottle claimed his 12th and 13th over France while working up for duty with the IAF in November 1918. Awarded the DFC and the Italian Silver Medal, he remained in the RAF (made MBE in 1920) and retired from the service in 1942 as a group captain, but was re-employed in 1944. He retired to India after World War 2 and died on 15 August 1967. Fellow ace Tom 'Voss' Williams remembered Cottle in my correspondence with him in the late 1960s;

'I was in many actions with Jack – he was more of a killer than most of us. He would have been just as happy fighting against us as with us! I will recount one action that was typical of Jack. We were following a leader who would stooge around but never close unless he had the enemy going away. This had been going on until he was as bored as I. One seven-scout formation that our leader had been trying to out-manoeuvre finally went down, then I saw them trying to overtake one of our RE 8s. Jack and I left the formation and attacked them, shooting down one each. Later, our patrol leader said he did not come down as there were only two Huns, and he didn't agree that there were seven. Nor did he confirm our kills, so we never got credit.'

Tasmanian Raymond James Brownell (born on 17 May 1894) also served in Gallipoli, with the artillery. Joining No 45 Sqn in France, he had 'made ace' by the time of the move to Italy. Here, Brownell added seven more kills to bring his score to 12. Whilst in the Army he had received the MM, to which he added the MC. Remaining in the RAF, he rose to Air Commodore CBE and died on 12 April 1974.

Nine Camel victories, plus two on Strutters, earned John Charles Bradley Firth an MC and Italian Bronze Medal. Born on 8 August 1894, it is thought he lived in London (his father's address was given as the Windham Club in St James's Square). Firth saw action over France and Italy, having joined the RFC in December 1916 from the 5th Battalion, KSLI, and he went to No 45 Sqn in April 1917. His

Capt C E Howell DSO MC DFC (left) claimed 19 victories with No 45 Sqn and Earl McNab Hand DFC, who scored five victories. Hand was shot down, burnt, and taken prisoner by the Austrian ace Frank Linke-Crawford, on 1 June 1918, but survived

Australian Capt R J Brownell MC claimed 12 kills with No 45 Sqn in France and Italy. His first victory was scored on his very first war patrol on 10 September 1917. Brownell later rose to the rank of air commodore in the post-war RAF

This view of No 45 Sqn Camel B2376 shows that the aircraft letter was carried on the top wing and the unit's dumbbell marking applied to the fuselage top decking. Aces K B Montgomery and R J Brownell both flew this machine in 1917 (*via R Lynes*)

Aces High! Peter Carpenter DSO MC and Bar (front) of No 45 Sqn is flanked by Harry K Goode DSO DFC and Charles M Maud DFC, both from No 66 Sqn. They claimed 24, 15 and 11 victories respectively

first seven Camel claims came in late 1917 over France, and especially during the Battle of Passchendaele, where he and others were involved in much ground attack work. Post-war, he worked for the Firth Steel Company, and died on 23 August 1931. Again Tom Williams recalled;

'One could write a book about John Firth. He was the most fearless man I ever knew, and perhaps the best pilot, but hopelessly inept at clearing stoppages with his Vickers guns. I owe my life to his fearlessness when I was shot down on one occasion. He stayed with me and fought seven German scouts. In another action over Italy, we shot down three enemy aircraft, and things seemed to be going well, but Firth signalled Tommy Thompson and I to break and head for the lines. As soon as he was over the lines he put his Camel down in some long grass, but waved me not to land. When he finally got back to base I asked what had happened. Both his guns had jammed, and he had landed to fix them, destroying his Very pistol hammering the cocking handles. As he had also seen five other enemy machines coming, he thought it better we should get out.'

Kenneth Barbour Montgomery, like Firth, only scored two victories over Italy, his other ten claims being achieved on Strutters (four) and Camels (six) over France. Born in Cheshire in October 1897, he won the MC for his actions over France. Montgomery became a flight commander in No 66 Sqn in January 1918, but after gaining his 12th victory he was shot down by ground fire and taken prisoner on 22 February. He received the Italian *Croce al Merito di Guerra*.

Mansell Richard James came from Ontario, where he was born on 18 June 1893. His 11 victories were all scored over Italy, for which he received the DFC. Ending the conflict in France as a captain, he was reported missing, presumed killed, during an air race on 29 May 1929. Other Camel aces to serve with the unit were N MacMillan MC with seven (of nine), P Carpenter DSO MC with eight (of 24), R J Dawes DFC, N C Jones DFC, E H Masters CdG (killed in a flying accident), H M Moody MC with eight, T F Williams with eight (of 14 – see No 28 Sqn), J H Dewhirst DFC CdG and E A L F Smith with seven, C G Catto, E D Clarke MC, A J Haines DFC (killed in action) and A Rice-Oxley DFC with six and F S Bowles, J E Child,

E McN Hand DFC and J W Pinder DFC with five, Pinder having an overall war total of 17.

The squadron's veteran CO, Awdry Morris 'Bunny' Vaucour, was born in south London on 8 May 1890. After serving in the artillery, he became an observer with No 10 Sqn in late 1915, then joined No 70 Sqn as a pilot on Strutters in 1916. Vaucour was credited with three victories with his observer, Lt A J Bott, whilst with No 70 Sqn, and both were awarded the MC. Vaucour was then given command of No 45 Sqn, and over Italy he claimed five victories to bring his score to eight. Tragically, he was accidentally shot down and killed by an Italian fighter pilot on 16 July. By then Vaucour had received a Bar to his MC, the DFC and the Italian Silver Medal for Military Valour.

Scotsman Norman MacMillan had been in the Highland Light Infantry prior to joining the RFC. With two Strutter victories and seven on Camels, he received the MC and became a flight commander. All his claims came in France, and although he went to Italy, he suffered facial burns in an accident and did not see further action. MacMillan later received the OBE and AFC, being Lord Lieutenant of Cornwall in later life. Born in Cardiff on 6 December 1892, Peter Carpenter had been a milling student prior to joining the RFC in January 1917. He scored his first eight victories with No 45 Sqn in France and Italy, then, going to No 66 Sqn as a flight commander brought his total to 24 by war's end. Awarded the DSO, MC and Bar, together with the Italian Bronze Medal.

Henry Moody, from Shropshire, scored half his victories in France and the other half in Italy. Winning the MC, he returned to England in June 1918 and remained in the RAF post-war. He was killed in a flying accident on 23 April 1931 when his Tiger Moth suffered a mid-air collision with a No 43 Sqn Siskin.

James Dewhirst had spent most of the war in the RNAS, but joined No 45 Sqn in Italy in 1918. He claimed six kills in the latter theatre, and his seventh, and last, victory over France on 5 November, these successes earning him the DFC and French CdG. Emerson Smith from British Columbia scored his first victory in a Strutter, followed by six more in Camels over France. He was then wounded in combat and taken prisoner following an engagement with *Jasta* 3 on 26 October 1917. Edward Clarke likewise gained a kill on Strutters and five more in Camels over France, winning the MC. He too was wounded by flak on 26 October 1917. Post-war, Clarke was Managing Director of Saunders-Roe Ltd on the Isle of Wight for a number of years.

Earl Hand, from Ontario, served with the Army prior to joining the RFC. After scoring five kills, he was downed in flames by the Austrian ace Frank Linke-Crawford on 1 June 1918 and was lucky to survive, burnt but a PoW. Post-war, he helped to form the Toronto Flying Club and became a magistrate. He died in 1954, aged 57.

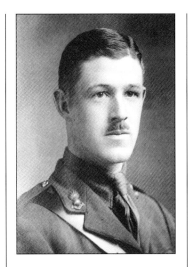

Maj Awdry M Vaucour MC and Bar DFC claimed five victories (to add to his previous three with No 70 Sqn) whilst serving as CO of No 45 Sqn in Italy. He was accidentally shot down and killed by an Italian pilot on 16 July 1918 (*via R Lynes*)

Camel B6238 was used by No 45 Sqn ace H M Moody to score five victories during the second half of 1917. Fellow ace Earl Hand then shot down a brace of Albatros Scouts with it on 11 January 1918 (*via Jeff Jefford*)

Canadian Gerald A Birks MC and Bar claimed 12 victories with No 66 Sqn, two of whom were Austrian aces Josef Kiss and Karl Patzelt

Pilots from Nos 28 and 66 Sqns pose for a group photograph at Grossa, in Italy, in the early summer of 1918. They are, from left to right, unknown, J Mackereth (six kills), unknown, P Wilson (seven kills), G F M Apps (ten victories with No 66 Sqn), H B Hudson MC (13 kills), unknown and S Stanger MC DFC (13 kills). The remaining four pilots are all unknown (*Bruce/Leslie collection*)

John Pinder we met in an earlier chapter, having gained 12 victories with the RNAS on Triplanes and Camels. All five of his claims with No 45 Sqn came after the unit had returned to France in late 1918.

No 45 Sqn's unit markings took the form of a white dumbbell on the fuselage aft of the roundel, which was repeated on the top of the fuselage. At first individual markings consisted of letters in front of the roundel for 'A' and 'C Flights' and numbers for 'B', but this changed to all letters by the time the unit had moved to Italy. These letters also appeared on the top wing to the left of the centre section cut-out.

No 66 Sqn

The third Camel unit in Italy was No 66 Sqn. Formed in June 1916, it went to France the following March with Pups and remained there throughout the summer, except for a few weeks on Home Defence duties from mid-July. The squadron received Camels in October 1917, and then came the move to Italy, where it remained for the rest of the war. In all 250+ victory claims were made, giving 19 pilots ace status.

William Barker and Peter Carpenter, both of whom we have met earlier, scored 16 of their victories with the squadron out of their totals of 50 and 24 respectively. Next came Harry King Goode, from Handsworth, born in 1892, although he later lived in Nuneaton. He served three years in the Royal Engineers and joined the RFC in late 1917. In Italy with No 66 Sqn, Goode accounted for ten aircraft, to which he added five balloons in late October 1918. He received the DSO and DFC. Staying in the RAF post-war, he retired as a Group Captain AFC in 1941, and was then employed as a civilian with the Accident Branch of the RAF. Goode was killed as a passenger in a No 120 Sqn Liberator when it crashed on 21 August 1942.

Francis Stanley Symondson, from Kent (born in Sutton, Surrey, on 27 March 1897) had also seen long service in the Army overseas with the Glamorgan Yeomanry. Transferring to the RFC, he first flew with No 29 Sqn, but his poor showing led him to be returned for further training after 16 days in France! Symondson obviously improved considerably, for with No 66 Sqn in Italy in 1918 he scored 13 kills and won the MC and Italian Bronze Medal, as well as becoming a flight commander. He continued flying privately after the war and died on 1 May 1975.

Canadian Gerald Alfred Birks was born on 30 October 1894 in Montreal. Flying with No 66 Sqn in Italy, he received the MC and Bar for his 12 victories. Included in his tally were Austrian aces Josef Kiss (19 victories) on 24 May and Karl Patzelt (five) on 4 May. Birks died in Toronto on 26 May 1991.

Charles Midgley Maud from Pool, Leeds (born on 1 April

1896) initially served in the Royal Field Artillery from May 1915 to July 1917. Fed up with this branch of the service, he moved to the RFC in 1917 and in 1918 found himself a Camel pilot in Italy. Maud's 11 victories won for him the DFC and Italian *Croce di Guerra*.

Gordon Frank Mason Apps came from Kent, where he was born in 1899. Joining the RFC in the summer of 1917 once old enough to do so, he gained ten kills and the DFC before being wounded on 16 July.

Another Canadian, from Toronto, was Hilliard Brooke Bell (born in January 1897). After serving in the Canadian Field Artillery he transferred to the RFC and flew with No 66 Sqn in Italy. He claimed ten victories and won the MC and Italian Bronze Medal. Bell died on 16 September 1960.

Other Camel aces in No 66 Sqn were C McEvoy DFC (9), H R Eycott-Martin MC and W M MacDonald DFC (8), A Jerrard VC (7), A Paget DFC and W C Hilborn DFC (6), H K Boyson and J S Lennox (5).

Christopher McEvoy from North London was lucky to survive one of his first combats in February 1918, being slightly wounded, but he went on to win the DFC. In World War 2 he served in Coastal Command. His brother was Air Chief Marshal Sir Theodore McEvoy. Harold Eycott-Martin won the MC with No 66 Sqn and gained eight victories, after serving with the Royal Engineers in 1915. William Hilborn from British Columbia gained a seventh victory with No 28 Sqn, but died of injuries ten days after a crash on 16 August 1918.

Alan Jerrard was the squadron's most unfortunate pilot. Born on 3 December 1897 in Lewisham, south London, he served in the 5th South Staffordshire Regiment before transferring to the RFC in 1916. In 1917 he was flying SPADs with No 19 Sqn but was injured in a crash on 5 August. Upon recovery he went to No 66 Sqn in Italy and claimed four victories between 27 February and 21 March. Then, on 30 March, Jerrard was in a three-man patrol with Carpenter and Eycott-Martin, and following a dogfight over the Austrian lines he failed to return. His two companions reported the action to their CO, and somehow a somewhat exaggerated story evolved and was passed on to HQ. This resulted in the award of the Victoria Cross for Jerrard – the one and only ever awarded to a pilot flying a Camel.

The report said 19 enemy aircraft had been engaged, although today it is known that only four were in the action! Carpenter claimed one kill and Eycott-Martin two, and they in turn told their CO that Jerrard had fought like a demon and shot down three before going down himself. Jerrard, of course, never put in any claims, and on returning from prison camp after the war stated that he had shot up one enemy machine and fired at some others but without being sure of any hits. One Albatros pilot had to land with a bullet through his fighter's coolant pipe, and another suffered a slight wound in the foot.

Jerrard's VC was announced while he was a PoW and it must have surprised him no end. The fight had ended when Jerrard was shot down by Austrian ace Benno Fiala von Fernbrugg, CO of *Flik* 51J. After the war Jerrard served in Russia and remained in the RAF, but only rose to flight lieutenant rank before poor health forced him to retire in 1933. He died on 14 May 1968.

APPENDICES

TOP CAMEL ACES

Name	Unit/s	Score
Capt D R MacLaren	46	54
Maj W G Barker	45/66/139	46 (50)
Maj J Gilmour	65	36 (40)
Capt W L Jordon	8N/208	39
Capt H W Woollett	43	35
Capt F G Quigley	70	33
Capt A H Cobby	4 AFC	29
Capt J S T Fall	3N/9N	28 (36)
Capt C M McEwen	28	27
Capt L H Rochford	3N/203	26 (29)
Capt P Carpenter	45/66	24
Capt S M Kinkead	1N/201/47	24 (35)
Capt A H Whistler	80	23
Lt Col R Collishaw	13N/203	22 (62)
Capt J L M White	65	22
Capt C R R Hickey	4N/204	21
Capt E J K McCloughry	4AFC	21
Capt G E Thomson	46	21
Capt A T Whealy	3N/203	20 (27)

Notes

N stands for Naval Squadron
Overall total in brackets includes all victories scored on other types

APPENDIX 2

SUCCESSFUL AIRFRAMES

The following list of Camels were those in which successful aces recorded victories, and therefore the machines themselves could be said to be 'high scorers'

Camel	Pilot/s	Unit/s	Score
B6313	W G Barker	45/66/139	46
D6402	H W Woollett	43	23
B9153	D R MacLaren/H N C Robinson	46	21
D3417	R Collishaw/L H Rochford	203	21
D6418	D R MacLaren/J Taylor	46	19
B6372	M B Frew/N C Jones/C G Catto	45	17
D1961	E J K McCloughry	4 AFC	17
B7220	A T Whealy/F C Armstrong/R A Little	203	16
E1416	A H Cobby/E R King/P J Sims	4 AFC	16
B6340	R J O Compston	10N	15
B7475	F G Quigley	70	15
B6344	J H Mitchell/N C Jones/P G Mulholland/J Mackereth	45	15
C8278	J Gilmour/H E Browne	65	15
D8118	J Gilmour/unidentified pilot	65	15
B6428	S W Rosevear	1N/201	14
B7190	W G R Hinchcliffe/S M Kinkead	10N/210/201	14
D1929	A H Cobby	4 AFC	14
C8270	J L Trollope	43	13
C1670	J Todd	70	12
D1898	O M Baldwin	73	12
B3858	G B Anderson/R M Foster	3N/9N/209	11
B3898	J S T Fall	9N	11
B6398	S M Kinkead/W R May/R T C Brading	1N/209/201	11
B7387	P Carpenter	66	11
D9394	C E Howell/A M Vaucour	45	11
E7279	M A Newnham	65	11
N6376	R R Soar/E G Johnstone/H T Mellings/D S Ingalls	8N/10N/210/213	11
B3858	G B Anderson/R M Foster	3N/209	10
B3884	A W Wood/M H Findlay	9N/201	10
B6426	A H Dalton/F C Gorringe	70	10
B7270	A R Brown/W R May/O W Redgate/J E Greene	9N/209/213	10
B9211	C J Marchant	46	10
C1615	D J Bell	3	10
C1627	G E Thomson/M L Campbell	46	10
E1417	L T E Taplin	4 AFC	10
F5941	G B Gates/R Sykes	201	10
N6370	A J Enstone/A J Chadwick/R M Kierstead	4N	10

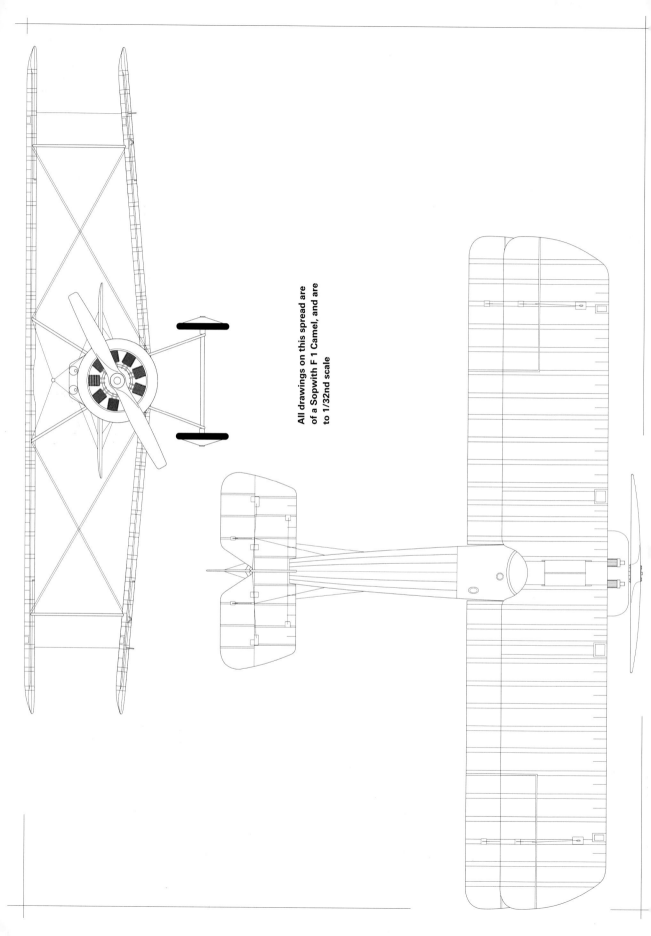

All drawings on this spread are
of a Sopwith F 1 Camel, and are
to 1/32nd scale

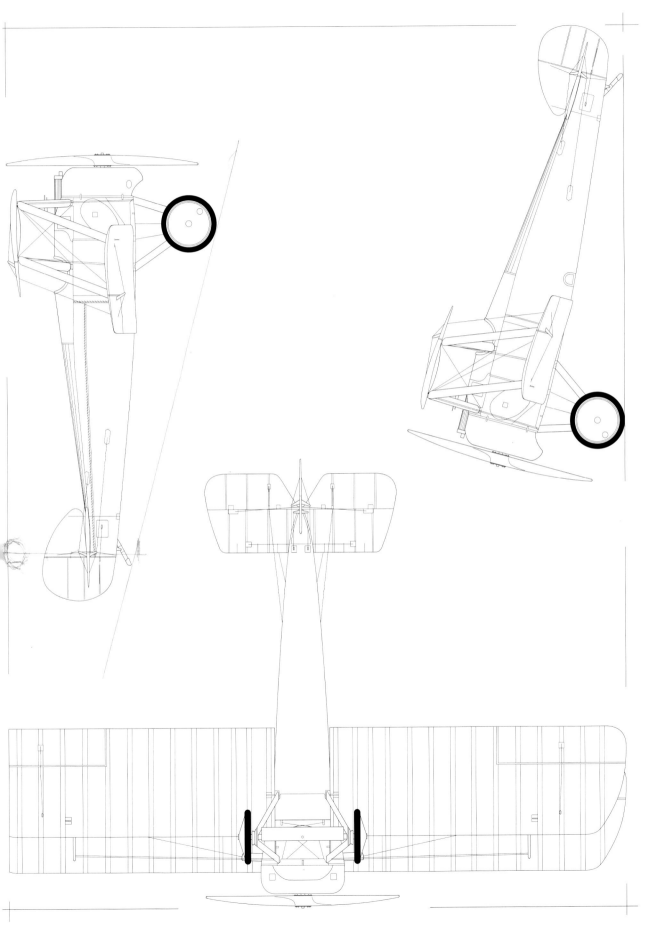

COLOUR PLATES

1

Camel F2153 of Lt G R Riley, No 3 Sqn, Valheureux, September 1918

This aircraft was used by Lt Riley while flying with No 3 Sqn, the ace claiming three kite balloons destroyed with it on 27 September 1918. The unit's Camel marking during World War 1 initially consisted of two vertical white bars behind the fuselage roundel, and this was officially changed to one bar either side of the cockade in December 1917, although it is not certain whether this was actually implemented 'in the field'. In March 1918 the markings were changed to two white bars behind the roundel. Flight marking was by coloured wheel covers – red, white and blue – while individual identification was by letters behind the cockpit for 'A' and 'C Flights' and numbers for 'B Flight'.

2

Camel B6344 of Capt J H Mitchell, No 28 Sqn, Grossa, November 1917

Capt J H Mitchell scored six victories with this aircraft in France and Italy between October 1917 and May 1918. Mitchell was 'B Flight' commander, and as such his machine carried pennants on the rear wing struts. The squadron marking was a white square aft of the roundel. In France B6344 had carried the number '1', which changed to 'G' in Italy.

3

Camel B6363 of Capt P Wilson, No 28 Sqn, Grossa, early 1918

Capt Wilson saw action in Italy, where he claimed five of his seven victories in this machine. The letter 'K' was stylised and the unit's white fuselage square is visible aft of the roundel. The letter and square were repeated on the top wing either side of the centre section cut-out.

4

Camel D8239 of Capt C M McEwen, No 28 Sqn, Sarcedo, late 1918

Capt McEwen claimed four victories in this machine, which was repainted soon after the end of the war in this vivid scheme. Note the unorthodox painting of the serial number.

5

Camel B5608 of Lt C F King, No 43 Sqn, Avesnes-le-Comte, March 1918

Lt King scored victories three to six with B5608 in February and March 1918. Its markings were standard for No 43 Sqn at the time, consisting of a white triangle aft of the fuselage roundel and an individual identification letter forward of the national marking. Flown by a deputy flight leader, the Camel flew a pennant from its rudder.

6

Camel B5620 of Capt H H Balfour, No 43 Sqn, Avesnes-le-Comte, Spring 1918

One of No 43 Sqn's flight commanders in the spring of 1918, Capt H H Balfour enjoyed some success with B5620 'A'. Indeed, he claimed seven victories with it in February and

March 1918. Note the leader's pennants fixed to the wing struts. The Camel's wheel covers appear to be white.

7

Camel D6402 of Capt H W Woollett, No 43 Sqn, Touquin, Summer 1918

Capt Woollett was No 43 Sqn's top scorer, and he flew Camel D6402 'S' between March and July 1918. When the machine still featured the unit's white triangle marking, Woollett had two white fuselage bands applied between the triangle and the tail. He later had white blotches painted all over the Camel as additional camouflage for when he undertook hazardous 'balloon busting' missions, but these were later ordered to be painted out. This profile depicts D6402 with the new squadron markings of two white sloping bars on either side of the roundel. The 'S' now appears on the top decking and not on the fuselage sides, the fin is marked with horizontal red, white and blue lines and the fighter's serial is worn on the rudder. Woollett's personal dragon marking was painted on both sides of the fuselage below the cockpit according to Jim Beedle's definitive volume on No 43 Sqn.

8

Camel B2430 of Lt E McN Hand, No 45 Sqn, Grossa, April 1918

This was the aircraft in which Lt E McN Hand claimed his first victory, in France, on 15 November 1917. R J Brownell then scored his first four victories in Italy with it, before Hand downed a further three in April/May 1918. A ninth victory was scored by another pilot after the machine went to No 28 Sqn.

9

Camel B6238 of Lts H M Moody and E McN Hand, No 45 Sqn, Istrana, January 1918

The mount of Lts H M Moody in France and Italy (five kills) and E McN Hand over Italy in January 1918 (two kills), B6238 was written off by Capt R J Brownell on 22 February 1918.

10

Camel B6354 of Lt J C B Firth, No 45 Sqn, Istrana, late 1917

Lt Firth used B6354 'N' to score three kills in late 1917, while Lt J Cottle gained his first victory in it over Italy on 10 March 1918. Other pilots also scored victories with B6354 prior to it crashing at Grossa on 25 March. At one stage the Camel boasted a white bar across the rudder, probably denoting where its serial number had been painted out and relocated on the fin.

11

Camel B6372 of Capt M B Frew, No 45 Sqn, Istrana, early 1918

Capt Frew had B6372 'H' as his aircraft in No 45 Sqn, and he used it to claim 12 victories, with C N Jones and J Cottle accounting for another five between them. As with all the unit's Camels in Italy, the dumbbell marking was repeated on the top decking. Individual letters were also marked on the top port wing outboard of the centre section cut-out.

12

Camel C1659 of Capt H G W Debenham, No 46 Sqn, Filescamp Farm, April 1918

This was the machine used by Capt H G W Debenham in March-April 1918, during which time he scored four of his six kills with it. Initially, No 46 Sqn's Camel marking was two white bars around the rear fuselage, with white letters aft of the roundel. However, from 22 March 1918 this changed to a horizontal white line mid-way along the fuselage, with individual letters immediately aft of the roundel.

13

Camel F2137 of Capt D R MacLaren, No 46 Sqn, Athies October 1918

Leading Camel ace Capt MacLaren used Camel F2137 'U' to claim his last nine victories during September-October 1918, boosting his tally to 54 kills. The 'U' was repeated on the top starboard wing outboard of the centre section cut-away.

14

Camel D8118 of Capt John Gilmour, No 65 Sqn, Bertangles, July 1918

Capt Gilmour claimed the last 14 of his 39 victories with D8118 during May, June and July 1918. Another pilot then claimed a 15th victory for the fighter. No 65 Sqn's Camel markings had originally taken the form of a white horizontal line along the middle of the fuselage, with individual letters behind the roundel. This was changed to a white vertical stripe either side of the fuselage cockade after March 1918, with individual letters in front of the leading stripe.

15

Camel B5181 of Lt M Gibson, No 66 Sqn, San Pietro-in-Gu, August 1918

This aircraft had begun its operational life with No 3 Sqn in France, where is was damaged. Once repaired, it went to No 45 Sqn in Italy, where Lt F S Bowles scored two of his five victories with it and Jack Cottle gained one of his. Lt M Gibson scored a fifth victory with the Camel in early August just prior to it being struck off charge. B5181's dumbbell is a little different to the usual squadron marking, and note that the serial has been applied both to the fin and rudder.

16

Camel B5649 of Lt Alan Jerrard, No 66 Sqn, San Pietro-in-Gu, March 1918

A winner of the VC with No 66 Sqn, Lt Jerrard claimed three victories with this machine in March 1918. His last action took place on the 30th of that month, during which he was shot down by Austrian ace Benno Ritter von Fiala and made a PoW. A glorified report by his CO in the wake of this mission led to Jerrard being awarded the VC.

17

Camel D8101 of Lt Gerald Birks, No 66 Sqn, San Pietro-in-Gu, June 1918

D8101 'P' was used by Lt Birks to claim his last two victories (taking his tally to 12) in June 1918. Lt G F M Apps then scored his eighth victory with it, while Lt W C Hilborn 'made ace' with D8101 in July. Two other pilots scored kills with the fighter before it was passed on to No 28 Sqn. No 66 Sqn's

markings were one vertical fuselage bar forward of the roundel and one horizontal bar aft.

18

Camel B3840 of Lt E C Gribben, No 70 Sqn, Liettres, August 1917

This machine was assigned to Lt E C Gribben in August 1917. Each flight within No 70 Sqn was identified by a letter, with individual numbers for the aircraft. Thus, this Camel was aircraft '4' of 'C Flight'. Gribben scored three victories with the scout, naming it *Pat 3*. During its brief frontline career, B3840 endured several collisions on the ground whilst serving with Nos 70, 46 and 66 Sqns, as well as being damaged in a heavy landing during its time with No 3 Sqn. The marking 'C' and '4' were painted in black on the undersides of the lower wing, with '4' being on the port side. No 70 Sqn's Camel markings initially consisted of white letters – 'A', 'B' or 'C' – aft of the cockade depending on which flight it was, and an individual number ahead of the cockade. This was then changed to a white zig-zag on the fuselage aft of the roundel, with individual aircraft letters between the cockpit and roundel. In March 1918 a further change saw three white vertical fuselage bands applied mid-way between the roundel and the tail, with the individual letters remaining the same.

19

Camel D9438 of Capt Emile Lussier, No 73 Sqn, Touquin, July 1918

French-Canadian Emile Lussier used Camel D9438 'D' to score his first three victories in July 1918. After being damaged in August, the fighter was rebuilt as H7226 in November. No 73 Sqn markings initially consisted of three white bars on the fuselage sides behind the roundel, and these were subsequently reduced to two white fuselage bands again aft of the cockade.

20

Camel B6313 of Maj W G Barker, CO of No 139 Sqn, Villaverla, August 1918

The most famous and highest scoring Camel of them all was Maj W G Barker's B6313, serving with him in Nos 28, 66 and finally 139 Sqns. Initially marked 'C1' and later 'N' in Italy, Barker finally had letters removed altogether and seven thin white bands applied around the rear fuselage instead – prior to the seven bands, it had carried just four, obliterating the serial number. Barker also had a red heart pierced with a white arrow painted on the fin. Another personal touch were the white 'notch' marks painted on the fighter's front wing struts for each victory. Finally, the Camel boasted a flat metal red devil on the starboard machine gun as a foresight!

21

Camel B7406 of Lt H G Watson, No 4 Sqn AFC, Clairmarais, May 1918

'W' was a part of No 4 Sqn AFC in 1918, usually being flown by New Zealander Lt H G Watson – he scored the first two of his eventual 14 victories with it. B7406 was damaged in a crash on 13 May 1918, and while rebuilt, it did not fly properly again. The unit marking of a white boomerang appeared on both fuselage sides aft of the roundel, and was repeated on the top decking.

22
Camel E1416 of Capt A H Cobby, No 4 Sqn AFC, Serny, September 1918
Capt Cobby scored at least nine victories with the 'serialess' E1416, Lt E R King claimed four more and Lt P J Sims gained three in early October to take the fighter's score to 16. By this time the squadron marking had changed to a single 'fat' white bar forward of the roundel, with individual letters aft of the roundel, repeated on the top starboard wing. Cobby had aluminium cut-outs in the shape of Charlie Chaplin screwed onto each side of the fuselage beneath the cockpit. One of these survives in the RAAF Museum at Point Cook, in Victoria.

23
Camel F6034 of 1Lt G A Vaughn Jr, 17th Aero Squadron, mid-1918
This aircraft was used by 1Lt G A Vaughn Jr to claim two victories on 22 September 1918, but in this same action the Camel was attacked by a fighter from *Jasta* 27 and written off in the subsequent crash landing, although the American was not hurt.

24
Camel E1537 of Lt Field E Kindley, 148th Aero Squadron, October 1918
Lt Kindley scored seven of his 12 victories in E1537 'B' in September-October 1918. It later served with Nos 45 and 151 Sqns in 1919. The 148th marked its aircraft with a white triangle, this identifier having previously been used by No 43 Sqn. Note E1537's red and white spinner.

25
Camel B3782 of Lts J A Glen and L A Breadner, 3 Naval Squadron, Bray Dunes, January 1918
B3782 was one of those Camels which flew with different units and pilots. Initially with 3 Naval Squadron, it was used by aces J A Glen and L A Breadner to score victories. The fighter then went to the Seaplane Defence Flight, which became 13 Naval Squadron, and that later became No 213 Sqn RAF. Taken over by Flt Lt/Capt J deC Paynter, he accounted for three German aircraft with it. B3782 was written off in a crash whilst with No 213 Sqn on 20 April 1918. 3 Naval Squadron's marking was two white fuselage bands aft of the cockade (or possibly one white band with a red line dividing it).

26
Camel B6401 of Lt L S Breadner, 3 Naval Squadron, Walmer, December 1917
Lt L H Rochford scored three victories with this aircraft in late January 1918. It then went to 8 Naval Squadron, then No 4 ASD, before ending up with No 213 Sqn, where Lt G C Mackay scored his tenth victory in it on 12 August. B6401 was deemed worn out by September 1918. Rochford's identification marks were a thick white vertical fuselage band aft of the roundel, with a white diamond shape on the top decking. Painted onto the diamond itself is a green maple leaf, as Canadian L S Breadner had earlier flown this Camel in the Dunkirk area. Breadner had 'sun rays' applied to the fin and elevators, but Rochford subsequently kept these on the fin only. Both men had the King of Diamonds playing card painted on the top surfaces of the lower wings.

27
Camel B6340 of Capt R J O Compston, 8 Naval Squadron, St-Eloi, February 1918
Capt Compston flew B6340 'P' with 8 Naval Squadron between November 1917 and February 1918, claiming 13 of his 15 Camel victories with it. The unit marking was a small white circle aft of the roundel, with the aircraft letter between this and the tailplane. With the introduction of aircraft letters, aircraft serial numbers were painted out, and it is unclear if they were marked on the rudder in all cases.

28
Camel B3883 of Flt Sub-Lt H F Stackard, 9 Naval Squadron, Leffrinckhoucke, September 1917
This was the usual machine of Flt Sub-Lt H F Stackard, who claimed four victories (and possibly two more) with it in September 1917. Two months later Flt Cdr J S T Fall scored his 30th, 31st and 32nd victories with B3883. Their Camel lacked a fuselage roundel, and instead had its individual identification marking applied in the form of a large circular band 'draped' over the fuselage in red, white and blue. Under the cockpit was the name *MAUDE II*, which is thought to have been applied in blue, with white shadow-shading. It is possible there were two Camels with similar markings, as another shows a slightly different sequence of ring colours (see additional profile on page 46). The Camel also carried two roundel-sized blue rings, edged in white, on either side of the centre section on the top wing, while the upper surfaces of the elevators were also blue with white leading and trailing edges.

29
Camel B3905 of Flt Sub-Lt A W Wood, 9 Naval Squadron, Leffrinckhoucke, September 1917
This aircraft carried the name *MURYEL* beneath the cockpit on its port side. During this period the squadron did not carry roundels on the fuselage sides, its aircraft instead being identified by various wide coloured bands around the fuselage. This machine was marked with what appears to have been a red and pale blue band, edged in white. B3905 accounted for four German aircraft, one of which was credited to A W Wood on 16 September 1917 for his sixth victory.

30
Camel B6230 of Lt F E Banbury, 9 Naval Squadron, Frontier Aerodrome, Autumn 1917
Flight Commander Lt F E Banbury flew B6230 with 9 Naval Squadron in the autumn of 1917, scoring five victories with it. Again, no fuselage roundels appear, the aircraft's individuality being marked by a thin diagonal fuselage band in red, edged in white, with the serial on the fin. The name *RETA IV* appeared just aft of the port-side cockpit edge.

31
Camel B7270 of Capt Roy Brown, No 209 Sqn, Bertangles, April 1918
This aircraft was famous because it was the machine that Capt Roy Brown used to chase Baron Manfred von Richthofen over the Somme on 21 April 1918 – a flight from which the Baron did not return. Brown was already a veteran of air combat by then, scoring his 7th, 8th and 9th victories in B7270 in March and early April 1918. Having fired at the

Baron's Dr I, upon landing Brown was told that he had shot it down, and he was credited with a tenth victory. The Camel was then flown by Capt O W Redgate, who scored two victories with it later that month. The machine later flew with No 213 Sqn, where Capt J E Greene gained three victories on 4 October and one more on the 14th. With No 209 Sqn, the Camel carried three white bars on the fuselage sides, one ahead of where a roundel might have been, and two aft. A red chevron, edged in white, appeared on the top wing across the centre section.

32

Camel B5663 of Flt Lt W A Curtis, 10 Naval Squadron, Teteghem, late 1917

Flt Lt Curtis used this aircraft to secure his 11th victory in late 1917. On 23 January 1918 it was in collision with an Albatros Scout and lost, its pilot Flt Sub-Lt Blyth being killed. The German pilot was also killed, although he was credited with the victory. Although reported to have fallen locked together, they appear to have separated near the ground, and this Camel landed pretty well intact. As an aircraft of 'A Flight', it carried this letter aft of the cockpit, and the forward stripes were black and white, as were the wheel covers.

33

Camel B6289 of Flt Lt W M Alexander, 10 Naval Squadron, Teteghem, January 1918

This aircraft was used by Flight Commander Flt Lt W M Alexander to score his second Camel victory (and his 13th kill overall) on 23 January 1918. This was the Camel's third success, Flt Sub-Lt H L Nelson having downed two aircraft in 1917. It then went to 9 Naval Squadron, and eventually back to England, where B6289 was destroyed in a crash in June 1918. Another 'A Flight' machine denoted by the 'A' by the cockpit, the fighter boasts a black star on its white wheel covers. Each Camel had differing motifs on their wheel covers as a personal identification marking.

34

Camel B6299 of Flt Lt N M MacGregor, 10 Naval Squadron, Teteghem, late 1917

Flt Lt MacGregor gained his last two victories with this aircraft in late 1917. It then briefly served with 9 Naval Squadron, before being passed on to a training depot at Chingford. As a 'B Flight' aircraft, it was identified by the 'B' aft of the cockpit and red and white stripes over the forward area and cowling, and in this case, on the top decking aft of the cockpit as well.

35

Camel B6358 of Flt Sub-Lt L P Coombes, 10 Naval Squadron, Treizennes, Spring 1918

Coombes used B6358 to gain his first two victories. It had previously been on the strength of the Seaplane Defence Flight, where Flt Sub-Lt J E Greene had destroyed a balloon with it and had then force landed on 4 December 1917. Going to 9 Naval Squadron, the Camel had been used by FSO M S Taylor to drive down a DFW in January, and after its spell with 10 Naval Squadron, B6358 went to No 213 Squadron. Here, Lt G D Smith shared a victory on 7 July. It was lost on 25 August 1918. With 10 Naval Squadron, the Camel featured the unit's blue and white stripes, reaching back to the cockpit.

36

Camel F5941 of Capts G B Gates and R Sykes, No 201 Sqn, Nouex-les-Auxi, Summer/Autumn 1918

Aces Capts G B Gates and R Sykes both flew this machine with No 201 Sqn, Gates claiming nine of his 16 victories in it during the summer of 1918, and Sykes downing his sixth victory with the Camel on 9 November 1918. Squadron marking consisted of a single vertical white bar aft of the roundel with individual letters between the cockpit and the roundel for 'A' and 'B Flights', and numbers for 'C Flight', while wheel covers were red, white and blue respectively.

37

Camel D3417 of Maj R Collishaw, CO of No 203 Sqn, Allonville, Summer 1918

Collishaw achieved 19 kills with this aircraft between June and September 1918. However, Capt L H Rochford had claimed two victories in it before Collishaw made it his personal Camel, and after the ace left the unit it may have been flown by Maj T F Hazell (the new CO), although he did not see combat. D3417 had a large white fuselage band aft of the roundel, and like Rochford's previous aircraft, this band joined a white diamond on the top decking. A white circle aft of this band was Collishaw's identification mark. No 203 Sqn markings applied after the Camels arrived, and after March 1918, consisted of a white circle aft of the cockpit. Individual markings were by personal mark or emblem on the fuselage, while flight markings were blue, red or black cowlings.

38

Camel D3332 of Capt E Swale, No 210 Sqn, Eringhem, September 1918

Swale gained four of his 17 kills in D3332 during September-October 1918. When he left on rest it was taken over by new CO, Maj W A Carter, who flew it in the last weeks of the war. In Swale's hands it carried a single white band aft of the fuselage roundel (over the fuselage but not beneath it) and a small white circle behind this. It also carried wing and tail streamers of black, yellow and red.

39

Camel D3332 of Maj W A Carter, CO of No 210 Sqn, Boussiéres, November 1918

When Maj Carter took over D3332, he had the fuselage re-painted with his initials applied in stylised letters forward of the roundel, while a dumbbell was painted aft of the roundel. A new serial had to be painted on too, as the one in the white rectangle had been overpainted. The letter 'A' was on the top wing starboard of the centre section. D3332 had had a long career. Initially with 9 Naval Squadron, it then went to No 204 Sqn, where Capt G H D Gossip had claimed his fourth victory in it on 20 May 1918, Lt C P Allen had gained his first with it on 29 June, and another pilot had scored a victory on 31 July.

40

Camel F5914 of Capt H T Mellings, No 210 Sqn, Teteghem, July 1918

F5914 was flown by Capt H T Mellings in July 1918, and he claimed his last four kills with it. He gained the last two on 22 July, but was killed in action on this date, shot down by ace Lutz Beckmann of *Jasta* 56 (his fourth of eight victories).

INDEX

References to illustrations are shown in **bold**. Plates are shown with page and caption locators in (brackets).